"You miss 100% of the shots you don't take."

— **Wayne Gretzky**

CASH FLOW FOR LIFE

How to Generate
an Income Online

JON MAC

CASH FLOW FOR LIFE
How to Generate an Income Online

Published by:
Crown Media & Printing, ID, USA

Jon Mac
www.CashFlowForLife.co
www.JonMac.co

ISBN: 978-0-692-73296-0

Editor: Julia T. Willson
Cover Designer: John Walter
Interior Book Layout: John Walter
Author Photo: Neil Slattery

Every attempt has been made to properly source all quotes.

First Edition

4 6 8 10 12 14

DEDICATION

To my father, who taught me how to always provide value to others first before asking for anything.

To my mother, who was always there for me, even in the hardest of times and gave me sound advice to continuously push forward.

To my brother Brett, who always knows how to have a good time in life and business.

To my Jacqueline, for inspiring me to stay focused and achieve my biggest life goals, dreams and aspirations.

"Every strike brings me closer to the next home run."

— Babe Ruth

ACKNOWLEDGEMENTS

I've been fortunate to network with some of the smartest individuals in the industry. Their concepts, ideas, knowledge, and strategies have helped shape my success path in life.

I have completed a number of training courses to boost my expertise in the digital marketing arena and it would be impossible to thank everyone who has helped me. But I do want to make an honorable mention of these genius marketers who helped me get to where I am now (in no particular order).

Simon Alexander, Thomas Bartke, Vlad Bretgoltz, Demian Caceres, Mo Ali Aguel, Mike Cooch, Emma Fong, Tim Keele, Nicholas Kusmich, Phil Kyprianou, Rory McDowell, Kaleb Phillips, Flavio Quaranta, Chris Record, Lowell Rempel, J.R. Salem, Will Schenk, Matt Schmitt, Shaun Spellman, Logan Thompson, Robert Walden, Don Wilson, and everyone else who has mentored me in some form or fashion during the past five years!

Last but not least, I'd like to thank my amazing team for

all the hard work, focus, and dedication they put into the business daily. Without them, the machine would seize up and there would be no cash flow. Thank you for putting up with my antics and becoming true friends in business and in life.

Paul, for managing our daily operations; Chelee, for managing our customers' satisfaction; and Al, for making sure our orders get delivered on time.

All your outstanding efforts have made this book possible.

CONTENTS

BONUS REPORTS

"Your time is limited, so don't waste it living someone else's life."

— **Steve Jobs**

Why Read This Book?

There are moments in your life that direct your destiny. These choices that you make are pivotal to your success. Moments come and go, but it's your job to choose which ones to hold onto tightly before they pass by. While many books have influenced my way of thinking, many others were all hype and no substance. It is important to keep learning and moving forward, but it's hard to find accurate information about e-commerce, as it is still such a new industry.

This is an exciting time! Every day brings newly discovered, cutting-edge marketing techniques. The opportunities are endless in this relatively unknown business model. Our parents didn't grow up with the Internet or the ability to target millions of people and sell products online.

In the future, I believe having an online store will be commonplace. We are in the golden age where we now have the technology, but it's still a big secret. There is less competition and greater rewards.

I wrote this book with the intention of not only being inspirational, but also practical. For me, this is one way to compile my knowledge and give back to the next generation of entrepreneurs.

Hopefully for you, this is one of those pivotal moments that spark a change in your life. Do NOT let it pass you by!

When I first started out years ago, I failed again and again and spent thousands of dollars testing what did and didn't work. Now you get to learn from my mistakes without making them yourself and gain access to all my proven results, case studies, and strategies compiled into an easy-to-follow book that you can read in a few hours.

Back in 2008 when the great recession hit, I was a real estate agent selling investment properties to wealthy individuals who were looking to diversify their portfolios with multi-family properties. After several deals fell through the cracks, I was left with $50,000 of debt and no career.

Turning to the Internet, I did what most of us do when starting out: I Google'd "how to make money online".

From there, my perception of the world completely changed. I finally understood that I didn't need to go to college, rack up huge debt, or work a 9-5 job and hope to one day get promoted to a management role just to work way more hours for a bit more money.

Stumbling onto several online marketing forums, I started learning methods and strategies to earn quick cash. Unfortunately, these methods were not stable, nor were they long-term.

What these experiences taught me was that it is possible to earn an income online. When I started using these methods, I was stunned to be earning $3,000-$4,000 per week! It was a huge revelation for me. With this newfound knowledge, I realized what was possible, and dug further into this world known as Internet Marketing (IM).

Networking with key individuals who were earning much more than I was at the time opened my eyes to more sustainable business models that could last for years instead of just a few days or weeks. Armed with this new perspective, I started testing frequently and learning firsthand the ins and outs of the e-commerce business.

I could never hold a job, either getting fired or quitting,

but something about running my own business was so exciting and special. I think that's the difference between a worker bee and an entrepreneur. The ability to never give up when times are tough, to break through the noise and focus on your successes.

As mentioned before, I didn't write this book simply to inspire you. There are already way too many books out there that do this. People are sick and tired of the "think and it shall become" philosophy. What you actually need is a playbook, a manual, a blueprint that actually works.

After coaching thousands of people on how to build, optimize, and scale their e-commerce stores, I realized that most are simply overwhelmed. They have too much outdated, useless, or confusing information that gets them nowhere.

This book was written just for you. It will show you the why, where, and how to create cash flow for life. It will get you on the right path to success without complications. The more you can simplify your business, the easier it will be to outsource and scale.

This book is full of actionable strategies to get you started on your e-commerce journey. Whether you're stuck on creating your basic business structure, choosing niches, sourcing products, or driving traffic, all will be revealed in this book.

What you have here is a full playbook to win! Never doubt yourself by wondering whether these strategies are going to work. Test them out for yourself and see how powerful they truly are.

Many mentors have coached me over the years, and I can honestly say that without their guidance I would not be where I am today. It's so vital to have a coach or mentor guiding you through the good times and bad. We all get stuck at some point in our lives, and it's important to put away our egos and ask for help.

I always say if you want something in your life, whether it's a new car or home or vacation time with your family, look at who has this success and reverse engineer them. I have put my knowledge, wisdom, and strategy into this book for you to take advantage of. My only hope is that after you read it, you will take immediate action to change your life!

This book will take you from start to finish. From setting up your store and launching your ads to exiting your business entirely and making 7 figures. You get all the strategies that I use in my own online business to earn a 7-figure income.

Through each phase, you will get a greater understanding about what it takes to sell more product, increase your average order value, and maximize your conversion rate. We'll explore each phase in detail throughout this book.

At the end of each chapter, you'll have the opportunity to immediately apply what you've learned to your own business by completing the Cash Flow Action Plan. If you answer these questions and complete these tasks as you read, you will have a fully functioning online store by the end of this book!

Finally, you'll receive my proven ad copy, niches, and even product examples that work in real life. No theory here. Instead, you'll find proven tactics to make you more money online without all the hype, jargon, and clutter.

Why am I sharing all that I've learned over the years in this book? Because I believe that once you hit a certain level of success in your life, it's your job to send the elevator back down. That is what I'm doing with you now. I'm giving you the opportunity I never had to find success more quickly than you ever thought possible.

I challenge you to execute on the strategies outlined in this book with passion and force. Don't take no for an answer. Push through your obstacles and never give up. You will find success even in the darkest of times. Follow through with your goals and win!

OPPORTUNITY OF A LIFETIME

When I was 15, I didn't have a clue what an entrepreneur was. Little did I know that I had already started finding my Entrepreneur DNA. It's interesting how our past life experiences influence our lives in the most unexpected ways. You don't know where life is going to lead you and how your skillsets will come together in a relevant way.

It all started in high school when I began hosting parties and DJing for my friends. As I held more and more events, my parties became more popular; some had 250-500 people. It was a ton of fun and I made a bit of cash at the same time, but this seemingly frivolous pastime actually helped me build skills for understanding an audience and performing on stage. It also gave me the confidence I needed later in life to succeed.

When I was 19, I was selling $3,000 vacuums door-to-door. This was my first real taste of being an entrepreneur. It was a tough gig. Visiting 4-8 homes per day, trying to get into a stranger's home to pick up dirt on their carpet in the hopes they would be grossed out enough to buy a vacuum.

For every vacuum I sold, I kept $1,000 commission. So when I did actually sell one, it was a big deal. I began to get obsessed with this "sales high" and loved it when I closed deals. But with every sale came even more rejection. This experience helped me develop a thick skin early on in life.

I don't think I ever dreamed of being in sales or even knew what career I wanted. I had a number of failed job experiences including Dairy Queen, where I'd invite my friends for free ice cream, and working at the supermarket in the seafood section, where I'd stuff myself with shrimp. I was fired from both those jobs.

I was by no means a model student either. I believe that school, though important, is not everything. You'll often find that children who are troublesome at school are actually bored. School trains you to follow rules. To obey a boss.

At the age of 21, I had finished university with no degree. I was a bit more educated on paper but still lacking a career path. If you are currently in school or college, I definitely recommend you finish your degree, but I don't believe that simply having a degree is the key to success.

I desperately needed a change from conventional education, something more hands-on. My parents knew I had sales skills and pointed me in the direction of real estate. So I began my journey to become licensed as a Realtor.

Within months, I had passed the exam and starting putting myself out there to get clients. Luckily, I got my first few deals from family and friends. But as time went on, I started to understand that I was working for free most of the time, as the average homebuyer looked at 10-20 properties or more before buying. Months would go by with no commission check, so my income was highly inconsistent.

I started to specialize my efforts to help investors find multi-family properties such as duplexes and 4-plexes. It was a fantastic learning experience, where I saw how real business owners operate with their investments and portfolios. I began to realize that emotions have no place in business and that numbers simply don't lie.

Today, in my early 30s, I've been an entrepreneur in

some form for more than 15 years. During this time, I've made many mistakes and spent hundreds of thousands of dollars on my education, whether that was buying training courses, getting mentorship with a coach, or spending money on my own testing.

The point is, you learn from each mistake and gain experience each time you fail. I never regretted anything in my business career because every occurrence was a valuable learning experience.

After 2 years of online marketing part-time, I finally went full-time in 2010. Quitting my job was one of the most satisfying experiences I've ever had. Although I am grateful to have had 9-5 jobs, I never quite fit in with my colleagues and managers.

If you feel like the routine is killing you, your mind is wandering, and your coworkers seem small-minded, you might be feeling exactly how I felt. It was hard to connect with people who were so motivated by the corporate ladder. They wanted things I didn't want, such as promotions, awards, and recognition.

I didn't care about those things. I wanted to build my own assets. My own company. I didn't want to spend my life building someone else's vision. I had my own.

As an author, speaker, coach, and mentor, I've had the opportunity to help thousands of people find their entrepreneur DNA and build profitable businesses. I've created products at a variety of different price points so people can get started on their entrepreneurial journey.

People ask me all the time, "If you had to start all over again with no money and no assets, what would you do?" I tell them to read this book, because this is the exact blueprint of what I would do.

I know you probably have many questions and I'm willing to answer them for you personally; however, in the meantime, you'll find many of the answers within this book, including actionable checklists and formulas to get your business off the ground and headed in the right direction.

This book has the power to change your life. The methods, strategies, and techniques in here changed my life for the better, and it will never be the same. But more importantly, it has changed my students' lives, again and again. It warms my heart when, after just 1-2 months, they tell me they've been able to quit their job, move to

tion, or get that dream home they always

n have anything you want in this life; you just need to want it badly enough. You need to obsess over this business and make it your life. You should dream about Facebook Ads and products and niches. I'm serious, because if you aren't 110% committed to making it work and breaking through your obstacles, you are less likely to succeed.

The key is to BELIEVE IN YOURSELF! Never give up. Stay focused and persevere! Entrepreneurship is a rocky road and it won't always be rainbows and lollipops, but the FREEDOM it gives you is unparalleled.

You will never have an opportunity like this in your life again. So jump in with both feet and get going! Now is the time to make a massive change in your life for yourself and your family.

"If you want what others have, you must do what others have done, and you will get what others have gotten!"

Reverse engineering other people's success is the fastest way to your own. Now you have the absolute guide right here to help you win at the game of life. It doesn't matter whether you're 16 or 60, this business is simple enough for anyone to manage and the technology is getting easier every day.

If you'd like to schedule a call with me, go here *jonmac. co/apply* and I'll have my team set it up.

Entrepreneur DNA

Which of the following scenarios most resembles you?
You're at a 9-5 job. Your boss micro-manages you. You
work with zombies. You get no respect and low pay for
how much you bring to the company. You can barely pay
the bills each month. You get no rest from the constant
stress and anxiety of trying to figure out how you're going
to make ends meet. Your wages are too low, you're tired
and you don't want to take on another job. You want to
make real change in your life but you don't know what to
do.

Or... you're in school (high school, university) and are
worried about getting employment in today's struggling
economy. Your parents complain everyday about their
jobs, lack of income and worry about retirement. You
want to make a more plentiful life for yourself, but you
just don't see the path to success. Or... you're already an
entrepreneur and are making a decent income, but want
to scale up your business by 10 times.

Regardless of our age, race, religion, gender, or current status, we all seek out a better life. A life without worry, doubt, or despair. A life where you wake up each morning happy and ready to take on the day. This is why it's so important to understand why thinking like a business person is the key to your success.

I challenge you to dig deep and find your Entrepreneur DNA. We all have it somewhere inside us. It's our duty to bring it to the surface and focus on our strengths. Find your passion for business and make it your profession. Chase your own dreams, not someone else's.

You know the saying: "Tell me and I forget. Teach me and I remember. Involve me and I learn." - Benjamin Franklin. This book will get you involved quickly and easily. It's broken down in a step-by-step format like a blueprint to follow. So you can take massive action and get results fast. This is the best way to learn.

If you don't learn how to fish for yourself, you'll never find the success you desire! With so much technology at your fingertips, it's now easier than ever to have entrepreneur DNA. You can have your own e-commerce store up and running within days. In this book, you will learn how to fish for life.

It saddens me to see so many people struggling these days, with the gap between rich and poor growing wider each day. The middle class is getting wiped out and many people can't see the light at the end of the tunnel. You might feel like this. Like you're on a mouse wheel with no end in sight.

It's interesting to see the difference in mentalities from those who grew up wealthy and those who did not. Some people in both groups grow up with an entitlement mentality, where they think everything should be given to them on a silver platter.

Unfortunately, that's not how life works. You need to have grit. Real staying power to make a change in your life. Where you want it as badly as you need to breathe. Only then, after working hard and smart, will you see success.

If you study, learn, and apply the strategies outlined in this book correctly, you will become profitable quickly. Don't forget to check out all the bonus material at the end, such as "25 Hot Niche Products" and "15 Store Optimization Tips".

What will you actually get out of this book? You will learn

how to start generating an income online. Why having your own business is so important in this day and age. How to realize your dream life more quickly than you ever thought possible.

Ultimately, you will learn how to expand your horizons, never give up, think for yourself, and hit your goals. All it takes is dedication and commitment.

Are you ready to change your life? To finally get results online? To be the director of your own life and create your own destiny? If the answer is yes, follow the strategies in this book carefully and create the cash flow for life you've always dreamed about!

Are you ready to start? Great! Your journey begins now.

Chapter 1

KNOWING YOUR POTENTIAL

I remember how I felt the first time I died. Well, not literally died, but figuratively.

I was in a McDonald's drive-through on a Monday afternoon. It was raining and miserable and I felt terrible. Having $50,000 worth of debt, no income, and no career, I was helpless. Paying off credit cards with other credit cards and barely pulling enough together to buy a $5 Happy Meal…this sucked.

I was at an all-time low, and had to borrow money from my parents and even from my girlfriend. It was a sad and embarrassing time, but I promised to repay them as quickly as possible. I knew I had to make a huge change in my life if I wanted to get back on the track to success.

So I became obsessed with earning income online, as there was nowhere else to turn. The recession had hit hard, and jobs were being eliminated daily in every sector. I knew I had to find something other than a job where I could potentially be let go at any moment. I needed something sustainable, where I could work from anywhere.

I knew deep down that I could do it. I could be my own boss and be in command of my own income. I knew the potential was endless online, where I could reach so many people so easily. But what would I sell? A product? A service?

I tried everything. From pitching credit report offers to people on Craigslist to selling Wal-Mart gift cards on forums. Some of these methods worked from time to time, and I started to see how I could make around $100 per day. This was a regular income for most people. It was incredible, and I knew my true potential at that moment.

With much luck, I stumbled upon Teespring, a t-shirt-selling platform housing thousands of vendors who sold shirts in the most random niches. It wasn't too long before people started to see the power of this business. I jumped into the deep end with both feet.

When I started selling 30-50 shirts per week using Facebook Ads, I was ecstatic! I couldn't believe people were buying these shirts from me every single day.

As I started to pay down my debt with the profits from these t-shirt campaigns, I could finally see the light at the end of the tunnel. Each week, Teespring would pay out my earnings from the previous week. I would pay off the Facebook Ads and pay my graphic designer, then bank the rest.

Scaling up my campaigns, I began to sell larger quantities of shirts in massive niches such as sports. Looking back at it now, I wish I had pushed it even further, because it was a lot easier back then.

Selling 1,000 shirts per week was a huge accomplishment for me and I couldn't believe it! But I knew there was more to this business than just t-shirts. The competition started getting intense. More and more vendors started their shirt-selling career daily, flooding the market with copycats.

I also knew I wasn't really building my own business, because I didn't own the domain or customer list. Instead, I was actually building Teespring's business and brand. This irked me, so I began the search for alternatives.

Moving my business to a WordPress site that looked similar to Teespring's sales page, I kept selling shirts.

The problem was that the technology was anything but smooth. When you run a WordPress site, you need your own server, and a number of things can go wrong.

Fulfillment was a nightmare. Customer orders were delayed 3-4 weeks because they would fall through the cracks and get lost in the mix. There was no good way to track sales fulfilling orders with WordPress.

It was a complete mess, and my business suffered dearly. Getting chargebacks and having to pay out refunds worth thousands of dollars was not fun, nor was it profitable. Especially having to pay for Facebook Ads on top of that and other expenses.

WordPress was obviously not the solution. There had to be a better option out there, something that was the best of both worlds. There had to be something that gave me the ability to build my own brand and business, with technology that actually worked.

Networking with other like-minded entrepreneurs, I discovered Shopify, an e-commerce selling platform. This was the solution I had been searching for!

I launched my first Shopify store and offered my best-selling t-shirts. I found fulfillment through a different t-shirt platform that offered me far better margins.

The results blew me away. The functionality was seamless. Everything worked smoothly. My customers were getting their shirts within 7 days or less, and I was getting rave reviews. Everyone was happy; it was a win-win.

Now that my business was back on track, I began researching other types of products to sell online. I knew there was a plethora of items people would buy. So I started looking at the best-selling products on Amazon, and one item kept popping up again and again.

Bracelets, necklaces, rings, and earrings. Jewelry was hot! People were buying tons of jewelry on Amazon in the $10-$50 price range.

I took my best-selling niches and applied them to jewelry. The sales started pouring in. That's when I knew what my true life's potential could be.

Up Next: In the next chapter, you're going to dive into the three phases of the e-commerce business. You will then map out your success to the ultimate goal of creating a 7-figure store. If you do this right, you will have cash flow for life.

Cash Flow Action Plan

1. How many months of income do you need saved in order to feel financially secure?

2. How many years of income do you need saved in order to feel financially free?

3. How many hours would you like to work per week?

4. What are 3-5 ideas for products you could sell?

Chapter 2

MAPPING OUT YOUR SUCCESS

When I first started out in this business, I had "shiny object syndrome". I jumped from training course to training course, from mentor to mentor. I invested thousands of dollars into software and strategies that got zero results.

Eventually, after spending years and money testing what worked and what didn't, I finally started to get traction. Perseverance was paramount to my success. I never gave up! I kept on pushing until something worked.

The beautiful part about owning your own store and brand is that you control the entire funnel. You have access to your buyers list. The way your store looks, functions, and feels. Upsells, downsells, applications (apps). There is so much opportunity to grow your own store.

The moment you stop testing and learning is the moment you stop growing. Sun Tzu said in The Art of War, "Every battle is won or lost before it's ever fought." This could not be truer. You must plan and execute carefully in order to win. But if you don't take action, nothing will happen. So be careful not to get analysis by paralysis.

Are you ready to map out a game plan for earning 7 figures?

I'm going to show you exactly what I do in my online business to earn a 7-figure income. All I ask is that you are 100% present, focused, and committed to achieving your goals. Forget the shiny object syndrome. Don't follow any other training courses, coaches, mentors, or software while you read, study, and implement the strategies in this book.

I have spent hundreds of thousands of dollars testing these strategies in my own business to find out what works and what doesn't, which will shorten your learning curve drastically. Put these strategies to use quickly, following chapter by chapter, and you will get fast results.

Three core phases outline how I run my business daily.

Phase 1 – Foundation This is where we dive into business fundamentals. Setting up your corporation and your dream team (accountant, bookkeeper, lawyer). The basic business structure you need in order to build your store to a level where you could sell it later if you wanted to. We will also discuss your personal energy levels. Diet and fitness are important factors for peak performance. You need mental clarity to tackle business daily.

Phase 2 – Launch This phase is all about getting traffic and sales to your store. You will learn the value of Facebook Ads, including how to create, optimize, and scale them. I'm going to show you how I break campaigns out into smaller components for massive profitability.

Phase 3 – Scale This phase is my personal favorite. Here you will learn about advanced strategies such as outsourcing, email marketing, branding, funnels, and exit strategies. This phase will take your business to a whole new level.

Now be honest with yourself. Which phase are you currently in with your business? If you're starting from scratch, begin with Phase 1. If you already have an e-commerce store, start with Phase 2. But make sure to read through thoroughly, as you don't want to miss any gold nuggets. Are you earning more than $2,000 per day? Then you might want to jump right into Phase 3 and increase your business by 10 times!

Regardless of where you are with your business, I suggest you read every chapter in this book. You never know what you might be doing wrong or could be doing better. There's always more to learn or improve upon.

With this three-phase road map to success, you will experience steady growth, week after week. Set regular goals, and make sure they are realistic and attainable.

After your store is up and running and sales are coming in, make sure you're growing your revenues weekly and monthly. Growth is essential for your business success. If you decide to sell your business down the road, investors will want to see steady growth.

Each week, you should be generating more sales, higher profit, more customers, and greater value for your business. Maintain a long-term outlook. This process isn't get rich quick or overnight, but it's probably the closest thing to it.

Up Next: In the next chapter, you'll discover how to structure your business and build your dream team. Without this core structure, it will be impossible for you to start your business with confidence.

Cash Flow Action Plan

1. How much money have you spent on training courses and materials within the past year? What value and improvements have you experienced as a result?

2. What emails from marketers do you receive daily? Consider unsubscribing from most or all of them so you can focus on these valuable tools and suggestions instead.

3. Which of the three phases is your business currently in: Foundation, Launch, or Scale?

4. Commit and schedule 2-4 hours per day to work on your business by recording blocks of time on your calendar.

Chapter 3

BUILDING YOUR FOUNDATION

Would you risk your family for your business? Would you risk your home or other personal assets?

I hope you answered no, because the absolute core of any business structure is risk mitigation. The ability to separate business from your personal life and vice versa. Before you start anything, you need to set up some form of corporation (or corp, for short).

If you don't own a corp, you need one as soon as possible. The average price for opening a corp is around $1,000, and having one set up will protect you for years to come. Any lawyer worth their salt can open a corp on your behalf.

Corps differ from country to country. In America, limited liability corporations (LLCs) are quite popular and could be an option for you. Schedule a meeting with an attorney to discuss opening a corp. You will not regret it!

Having a sole proprietor business does not protect you. You are still personally liable for lawsuits and assets you own if something happens to your business. Imagine if the bank took away your home. How would your family suffer? It's simply not worth the risk.

I own several corps for my different businesses. Down the road, you might want to spread out your risk as well if you run multiple niche stores.

Let's not forget the huge benefit of paying much lower taxes when comparing corp income to personal income (for example, as a sole proprietor). In the US, federal tax rates on corporate taxable income vary from 15% to 39%. In Canada, expect to pay around 15% corp tax compared to 30-50% personal tax. That's a massive difference.

Also, you have the ability to write off a number of business expenses, which reduces your tax burden even further. Opening a corp is worth the effort for the tax savings alone.

Remember, a corporation is its own entity. It's like you created something out of thin air. It has no real relation to you other than the fact that you own it and can sell it, along with the business or store, in the future. It's much easier to peel off corps as an exit strategy than to have all businesses within one corp. (You'll learn more about exit strategy in a later chapter.)

Finding a knowledgeable and experienced bookkeeper can be the difference between truly knowing where you stand in your business and not having a clue. Ranging from $10 to $60 per hour, professional bookkeeping services will save you from many headaches in the future.

They will track your business income and expenses weekly or monthly and code them all into a chart. A basic knowledge of accounting is helpful for any business owner. (Estimated quarterly payments are still beyond me; that's why I have professionals take care of it all!)

Find a bookkeeper in your city whom you can meet with regularly, for example to clarify certain transactions they might be unsure about. It's a big plus to be able to meet with them in person. Get organized and your business will flourish.

Next, find a professional and experienced accountant. I highly recommend a Chartered Accountant or Certified Public Accountant (CPA). Seek out someone who has been accounting professionally for at least 5 years, but 10 years or more is even better. Do not hire a less-qualified person who has no official designation. Hire a professional who will keep you legal and save you money on taxes.

Taxes, like death, are a certainty we cannot escape in this life. But we can certainly reduce them as much as possible. If you dislike paying half your profits to the government, invest in a really solid accountant so you retain more money for reinvestment. Your accountant will have legal tax strategies to maximize your deductions and tax credits.

If you are not in the United States, set up a United States Dollar (USD) credit card and USD bank account. It's much easier to manage and scale your business if you keep everything in the same currency. For now, the world currency standard is USD and, because you will primarily be selling to the US market, it makes sense to keep everything in USD.

Also, try to obtain a high limit on your USD credit card. When you start scaling up your ad spend, you will need that extra room to push your campaigns harder. The more you spend, the more you make.

Secure a banking relationship with a business advisor so you have a contact if you ever need a credit limit increase or have to move money around quickly.

This whole book revolves around creating cash flow for life with a successful online business. But if you want this lifestyle, you need to know your numbers. This starts with tracking your income and expenses—money in vs. money out.

It surprises me how many entrepreneurs I coach who don't even track their daily profits or return on investment (ROI) properly. How can you determine the health of your business if you don't know your numbers? Start making it a habit to calculate your numbers daily, weekly, and monthly. This will put you on the right track for a successful business.

Finally, you must understand the difference between a lifestyle business and building a real asset. You might prefer to coordinate the day-to-day operations of your business, if that's what you're passionate about, and you might earn a decent amount of income from that. You can travel when you want and work when you want. However, unless you're there in the trenches, your business might not grow. In this case, you are essentially self-employed.

Compare this to building a true asset, where you step outside the business. Your project manager oversees the daily operations and manages the staff on your behalf. (Note: In a future chapter, we will cover this topic in detail.)

This book teaches you how to build a real online business, not just create another job for yourself. You will see how critical it is to focus your efforts on the tasks that bring in revenue growth. For example, customer service, fulfillment, and fan page management should all be outsourced as soon as possible. This will leave you open to focus on the most important income-producing activity, Facebook Ads.

Hire your dream team with great care, and select professionals who will help launch your business and keep it on track as you scale upward.

Up Next: In the next chapter, you'll explore personal performance and how it relates to your business success.

Cash Flow Action Plan

1. Do you want a lifestyle business where you are involved fully or an asset that brings in revenue on its own?

2. Identify potential accountants, bookkeepers, and lawyers you could hire to support your business.

3. Do you currently have $3,000-$5,000 in savings to fund your business?

4. If you answered "No" to Q3, can you use a credit card to get started? (You should easily have enough income before the statement arrives to pay off your account and avoid paying interest.) If not, establish a savings goal with specific target date.

Chapter 4

MAXIMIZING YOUR PERFORMANCE

How do you feel each morning when you wake up? Are you excited about what the new day has in store? Do you jump out of bed full of energy? Or do you sleep in whenever possible? Do you feel groggy and out of it? If you're in the latter category, it's time for a system reboot!

As an entrepreneur, it is absolutely essential for you to be healthy. Not just for your own well-being, but for the well-being of your business, employees, and overall growth. If you have a high sugar diet, you most likely are crashing hard several times per day, unable to focus on the task at hand.

Your diet is a critical component to being healthy. Eating right is the key to high energy, focus, mental clarity, and more. In a world where it's harder and harder to focus on tasks due to the overwhelming number of messages and social media sites competing for our attention, we need to allocate our time wisely.

It's too easy to grab a chocolate bar or bag of chips when you feel a bit peckish. Instead, I encourage you to grab an apple or banana or, better yet, kale chips. Being on a high sugar diet is detrimental to your health, and contributes to a toxic environment within your body.

Starting your morning on the right foot will set up the rest of your day for maximum performance. Try a protein shake, as it's vital to get protein into your system within one hour of waking. Mix in almond milk, berries, or bananas. (Never use cow's milk, unless you want antibiotics, hormones, and steroids in your system.) I highly recommend a green "super food" mix full of antioxidants. Chia seeds and flax seeds are also great for digestion.

Other than eating clean—which means including more fruits and veggies and fewer carbohydrates such as rice, bread, and cereal in your diet—portion control is equally important.

Be honest with yourself: Are you overweight? Could you stand to lose 10-20 pounds for a leaner, healthier you? I know I could benefit from losing some pounds. It begins with portion control. Try halving your regular portions at each meal, and watch how quickly you shed the fat.

Exercise is almost as important as your diet to keep your energy levels high and your mental game clear. Try working out for 15 to 20 minutes in the morning before you eat. You need to get your heart rate up enough for a high-intensity workout. I recommend sprinting then walking (on a treadmill or outside), then sprinting then walking, with a 10% incline and 1-minute intervals, for 20 minutes daily.

In Timothy Ferriss's book *The 4-Hour Body*, he recommends 75 kettlebell swing reps, 2 to 3 times per week. These efficient exercises will get you in shape without sacrificing too much of your time.

Finally, emotional health can have a huge impact on your business. Stress, anxiety, depression, lack of confidence, and mistrust can all lead to poor decisions. You need to be in control of your emotions so you are able to examine the facts with logic and not fear. Make sure you're in a good state of mind before you start your business and not in a state of desperation (especially financially), as this will set you up for failure.

There you have it. These are the small steps that can make a huge difference to your business performance. Without keeping your diet, exercise, and emotions in check, you will waste time, become distracted, and possibly burn out.

Up Next: In the next chapter, you'll learn how to reverse engineer the competition and find out what's working now in the marketplace. It doesn't get any easier than this!

Cash Flow Action Plan

1. Create 2-3 goals for the next 30 days related to your diet. (EX: avoiding sugary or diet drinks, processed food, or simple carbs)

2. Create a fitness goal (EX: waking up earlier to exercise or a target weight) that you can achieve in 30 days or less.

3. How will you ensure that you are emotionally healthy?

4. Make a specific plan to effectively manage stress and minimize its impact on your business. Enlist support from others as needed.

Chapter 5

Recreating Their Success

Are you ready to start constructing your online store? Reverse engineering is where to begin. In order to build a successful business, why not look at similar businesses that are already successful? No need to reinvent the wheel here. Take what works well, tweak it, and make it better.

Some e-commerce stores that are highly successful include LizzyJames.com, VictoriaEmerson.com, and LisaLeonard.com. You will notice what they all have in common: their domain is a person's name. This naming convention works well, as it represents a sense of luxury to your customers. I recommend using names like this to portray quality.

When you visit each online store, you'll see what works well for them. A large amount of white space and white backgrounds make the sites feel clean and welcoming. Also, notice how they use photos of models wearing their jewelry. Their images are top-notch and have a polished, high-end look. Their prices ranges from $20 to $150 per item.

I suggest you start around the $20 price point when you're just getting started or, better yet, the Free Plus Shipping model, which you'll learn more about later.

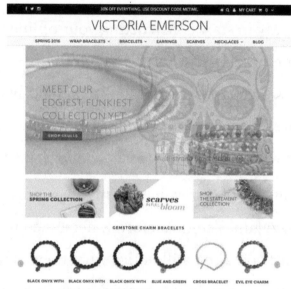

Figure 5.1 VictoriaEmerson.com home page

These stores have effective calls to action (CTAs), and site navigation is intuitive. Note the colors, fonts, and font sizes. Luxury brands typically use a smaller font. You might want to test this as well.

On the product page, Add to Cart is the most commonly used CTA. It has been proven repeatedly to convert the highest number of sales compared to Add to Bag or Buy It

Now.

But what are these stores missing? What are the elements that could bump their conversion rate (CR) by 1% or even 2%?

For one, a 24-hour countdown timer will easily increase the CR for your store by at least 1%, according to my own testing on several different niche stores. This is a simple timer you could use along with a teaser such as "Hurry before this deal is gone!" Scarcity greatly improves

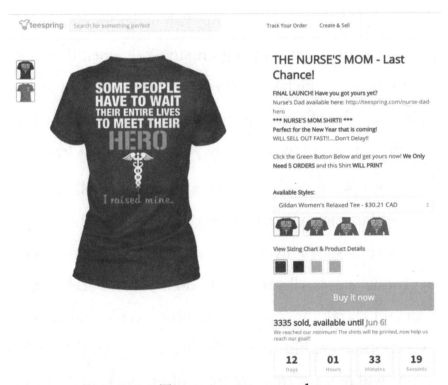

Figure 5.2 Teespring.com product page

conversion. Second, you could display on the product page the number of items that have been sold. Teespring does this well.

When you imagine what your first store will look like, consider a broad niche store. The advantage of having a domain naming convention such as LizzyJames.com is that you can theoretically put any jewelry product on the store in any niche. You will not be limited to, for example, just "gold" or "gemstone" jewelry. You will have free rein to test as many niches and products as you want.

The name of the game is testing. You never know what's going to work or what's not going to work when it comes to products and niches. So do your homework and test different styles of bracelets, necklaces, earrings, and rings in different niches to see where you get the most traction.

Next, find proven products that are working well in the marketplace. There's an easy way to determine this to significantly shorten your learning curve when it comes to product sales. All you have to do is access Facebook. com and search for "just pay shipping". You could also try variations of this, such as "only pay shipping". Search results will reveal a treasure trove of products in different niches that are doing well.

The "just pay shipping" strategy is a good way to get fast traction and start testing niches. As you sell products, you quickly begin to understand your audiences. You will learn that selling products is more about knowing who the passionate buyers are and finding or creating a product for them rather than creating a product first and then trying to find the buyers.

So how do you find the best-selling products in the newsfeed? Which products are selling well? That's easy! Just look at the number of Likes, Shares, and Comments

Figure 5.3 Facebook Ad post comments

on each post. The more social engagement on a post, the better. I prefer to scan for product posts that have more than 5,000 Likes, but 10,000 or 20,000 are even better.

Favorable comments also indicate that a product is selling well. Are people saying they bought the item, or just received it, or love it? This means sales are strong with this one and you might want to pursue the opportunity further.

The next question to ask is whether the product is easy to target. Can you clearly see how the vendor is selling the product on Facebook? Read the fan page name. What does it say? Can you figure out instantly what the niche is, just from reading the comments or the product description?

If you can, you have a winner. If you can't, you might want to skip this one, because it's probably a generic product that will require a great deal of time and money to sell. (The concept of targeting is covered in the chapters ahead, so don't worry.)

Next, check when the ad was posted. The date will display just below the fan page name on the post. If the post is only 2 or 3 months old, that's okay. Any older dates could indicate that the campaign is over and the product is tapped out, although that's unlikely if the niche is large enough.

Look at the most recent comments and see when they were added. If they were from today, such as 1 or 2 hours prior, then the vendor is probably still running the ad effectively. In this case, consider testing out the same product on your own store.

Finally, after you've collected 10-20 products to test, you need to figure out where you'll get them fulfilled (that is, sent to your customers). My suggestion is to source the products from AliExpress.com. There you'll find thousands of products to promote on your store.

After you find a product you want to test, a couple of steps must be taken.

First, I recommend that you only work with vendors on AliExpress that have blue diamonds on their profiles. This indicates that they are reputable and have a good overall rating.

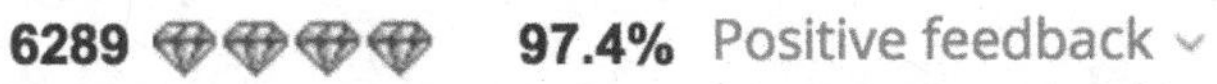

6289 💎💎💎 **97.4%** Positive feedback ⌄

Figure 5.4 AliExpress.com vendor feedback (blue diamonds)

Never work with vendors that have blue ribbons or other such badges. These are actually paid for by the vendors, and not true feedback.

293 🎗️🎗️🎗️🎗️🎗️   **98.7%** Positive feedback ⌃

Figure 5.5 AliExpress.com vendor feedback (ribbons)

Only blue diamonds…and the more diamonds, the better.

Second, check the price of the product including ePacket shipping to the US. If the total price is $3 or less, you're in luck!

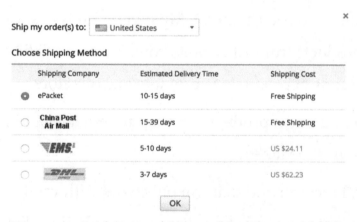

Figure 5.6 AliExpress.com shipping methods

When you open your store, always start with the Free Plus Shipping model, because it's the easiest way to get instant traction and really get your feet wet with Facebook Ads.

So if you charge the standard $9.95 for shipping/handling,

and give away the actual product for free, that's roughly a $9.50 margin after transaction fees (Shopify) before fulfillment costs. And if you factor in a $3 fulfillment cost (to order and ship the product to your customer), you are left with a $6.50 margin, which is excellent.

So $7 dollars is all you need to scale up to several hundred sales per day and hit an impressive ROI. At this rate, you'll start to see how powerful this method really is, because you are marketing the product as "free" where customers only have to cover shipping and handling. The conversion rate with this method tends to be particularly high, in the range of 5-10% from cold traffic.

Up Next: In the next chapter, you'll learn why optimizing your store conversion rate is so important for your profitability. This is key to understanding how to generate sale after sale with your store.

Cash Flow Action Plan

1. Which 10-20 proven products in the Facebook Newsfeed could you test in your store?

2. Identify 10-20 products on AliExpress that you can purchase and ship for less than $3.

3. Find and register a domain name using the personal naming convention mentioned earlier.

4. Locate a high-converting theme on the Shopify theme store that matches the look and feel of your competitor's stores.

Chapter 6

LAUNCHING YOUR STORE

I have launched many stores.

Let me clarify that. I have launched many failed stores.

When I first started out, I went a bit overboard with my launch. I decided that a niche store was better than a general store. This worked out okay at first, but I was quite limited with the products I could test. Not only that, I had too many stores to manage and couldn't keep up. I started losing money because of the organization and became overwhelmed.

It's better to start off with a general store and make it the best general store out there than to spread yourself out too thin and sacrifice quality.

I've made many mistakes, so to save you time and headaches, here's what you should do and not do.

After you've found several niches and products to sell, you're ready to begin launching your store. Offer a mix of retail-priced products and Free Plus Shipping products.

A mix of different price points is beneficial to establish trust with your customers. I suggest pricing between free and $49.95. This will help your store look legitimate, and improve your conversion rate and average order value, which we'll cover in later chapters.

Find and register a domain name using a personal naming convention; this works especially well with jewelry stores. It's also good practice to make your information private when registering your domain. After you register, connect your domain name to your store and create your first email address using the following template: support@yourdomain.com (EX: support@ fishingfun.com). This email will be used for all your customer service inquiries.

Learn how to set up your Shopify store in detail on their website under Initial Setup. All traffic should be redirected to [yourdomain.com] only. Another important point is to have the time zone of your store (EX: Pacific Standard Time/PST) set up to match your Facebook Ads account time zone.

For currency, it's best to collect in USD, as you will mainly be targeting US customers with your store. In terms of collecting money from Shopify, set up Shopify Payments, which essentially is a white-labeled version of Stripe's payment processor.

The fee per transaction will vary depending on the Shopify plan you choose. Fees start at 2.9% plus 30¢ per transaction. You will be paid out daily NET 3 (every 3 days) if you are in the US, and daily NET 7 (every 7 days) anywhere else in the world.

Shopify Payments will allow you to accept credit card payments for your store. PayPal is another payment option. However, I highly advise against using it unless it's your last resort and you cannot find another merchant account solution.

PayPal has frozen my funds many times and my friend's funds as well. One of my friends lost $60,000 to PayPal, and I doubt he'll ever get it back. Once you start making transactions more than $100,000/month with PayPal, they automatically put you on a rolling-reserve basis, which means they hold a percentage of your money for 3-6 months at a time.

It's also not worth the hassle of dealing with payment disputes from your customers because PayPal makes it so easy for them to Login and create a dispute. With Shopify Payments, your customers can only use their credit cards and it's much more difficult for them to complain if they're unhappy. So again, my suggestion is to avoid PayPal at all costs.

You have three options for your Shopify plan: Basic, Professional, and Unlimited. I suggest going with Professional, as it gives you a better rate (2.7% instead of 2.9%) and access to the Reporting feature in Shopify Admin, which is critical for tracking your sales daily, weekly, and monthly.

For your store theme, it's best to choose one that is elegant but also geared toward conversion. There are several high-converting themes I recommend under webdesigndev. com under "Shopify themes".

If you want to add a countdown timer on your product

Figure 6.1 Optimized theme with countdown timer

pages to increase your conversion rate, search on Shopify for "hurrify countdown timer".

Other top apps you might want to install in your store include:

- Abandonment Protector

- Buy X, Get One

- Google Shopping

- MailChimp

- Notify

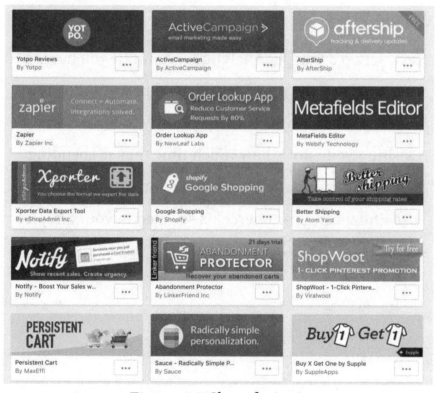

Figure 6.2 Shopify Apps

- Order Lookup

- Persistent Cart

- Receiptful

- RetargetApp

- Xporter

- Yotpo Reviews

I don't cover all these apps in this book because that would be a whole other book! But you can find out how they work by installing them on your store and playing around.

Next, set up a Google Analytics account (if you haven't already). Copy the tracking code and paste it into your Shopify store settings. This will allow you to see who is visiting your store, how much time they're spending on product pages, and your conversion rate. Make sure "Use Enhanced Ecommerce" is selected in your Shopify settings.

Figure 6.3 Google Analytics Shopify settings

You should have a phone number for your store so your customers can call and leave messages with their names, emails, and issues or questions. This will allow you or your team to handle customer service inquiries efficiently and give your store a credible look and feel.

I suggest getting a phone number with Grasshopper.com. The $24/month plan is acceptable and will give you enough minutes to handle incoming calls. To be clear, you will not be answering calls directly. Instead, calls will be routed to a voicemail account, and you can handle them from there.

For a professional sounding voicemail recording, consider having one created for $5 at Fiverr.com. This way, your message will sound legitimate like any other big box company and will really help in terms of customer retention.

Your voicemail recording could simply say: "Thank you for calling [yourdomain.com]. We are currently experiencing a high number of calls. Please leave your name and email address and we will respond within 24 hours."

Having your team handle customer service inquiries allows you to focus on the growth of your business.

For shipping rates, I prefer to use the Better Shipping app, as it allows you to create rates per product and even tiered rates (discounts for customers who order more than 1 or 2 items). It's simple to set up and use, so install it and become familiar with how it works. It will save you future headaches, for example when a customer buys a Free Plus Shipping item and a retail item in the same order.

Up Next: The next chapter is one of my personal favorites. Learn about what it takes to increase the conversion rate on your store so it becomes more profitable, month after month.

Cash Flow Action Plan

1. Which store theme are you going to use?

2. Which merchant account are you going to use? (Shopify Payments, Stripe, PayPal, or other)

3. Access Fiverr.com and record your professional voicemail message.

4. Set up shipping rates for every product in your store.

Chapter 7

OPTIMIZING YOUR CONVERSION

Want the sales to start pouring in? Your store conversion rate is the key. Once you understand how important it is to convert traffic into sales at a good rate, you will see your sales start to take off.

It all begins with having your store mobile-optimized because you will use Facebook Ads to drive traffic, and 80-90% of that traffic will be mobile.

Why is mobile traffic such a huge percentage? Because more and more people are using their phones to access Facebook and the traffic is cheaper and can be higher quality than desktop traffic.

You must ensure that your store is attractive, is easy to use, and has a quick checkout process on mobile devices. You can use Chrome browser plug-ins and websites to test your store on both iPhone and Android devices. Check that each device displays your store in the correct format and that the Buy button isn't too far from the top of the page, so people can easily find it.

The checkout process on your store should be seamless, so your customers can check out with just a few clicks. Three to four clicks are the most it should take to get them to the order form and input their credit card details. Any more clicks than this could seriously hurt your conversion rate.

On the desktop version of your store, make sure your Buy button is above the fold (that is, on the main page with no scrolling required) and test out a solid green color with white font at first. Green buttons have been proven time

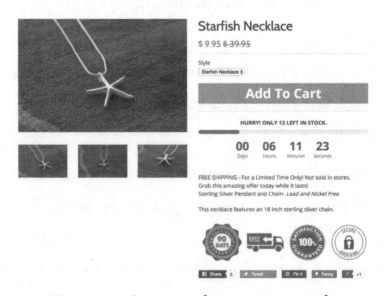

Figure 7.1 Store product page example

and time again to convert well. Use "Add To Cart" for your Buy button text.

Don't distract people from clicking around too much on your store. You will drive 90% of your traffic to a product page, which focuses on having people Add to Cart and check out.

So limit your navigation bar to a simple menu icon that visitors can click if they want to see the navigation bar. A black bar at the top of the page mentioning a promotion of some kind works well. Below that, add your logo and then below that, your product image.

Keep it simple and clean, with a white background and 1 or 2 other colors max. Always mention a promotion

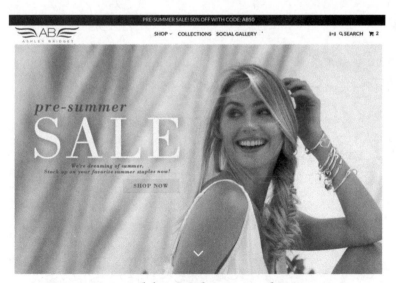

Figure 7.2 AshleyBridget.com home page

of some kind in the description, such as "50% OFF" or "FREE Shipping". Both work extremely well for retail-priced products.

Below the description, feature related products, which act as a cross-sell just in case people aren't interested in the main product. They can click to other similar products and buy them instead.

Finally, include a review section where customers can post comments and rate their experiences with your store.

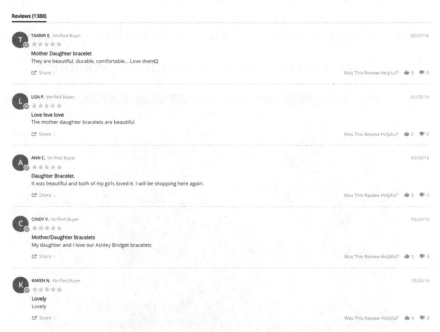

Figure 7.3 Yotpo Reviews app

My company has tested many types of carts and the version that's working best right now is a right-side pop-out cart. The user never leaves the product page, so this reduces the number of pages they need to use for checkout. Within just a few clicks, they secure their order. The fewer actions they take, the better.

Figure 7.4 Right-side pop-out Add To Cart bar

The checkout page itself should have some trust seals [EX: McAfee] and credit card logos to show that your store is credible and trustworthy. You can find examples on the Shopify site. Testimonials on the checkout page help to increase your conversion rate as well.

Design your checkout process to capture customers' email addresses before they reach the credit card form. This is essential for people who abandon their cart and don't purchase from you the first time.

Ask yourself, "Would I buy from my own store?" If the answer is no, go back to the drawing board and make sure your store experience is friendly, intuitive, and easy to use. The faster you get people through your funnel, the more profitable your business will become. Establish trust early on with all your ads, product pages, and email communications.

Every time you interact with a customer, your message should be consistent and professional. This will help with your branding and ensure that your store is considered a trustworthy place to shop online.

There are several other ways to increase your conversion rate. Scarcity, when deployed correctly on your product pages, can bump your conversion rate immensely. By simply adding a countdown timer that resets every 24 hours, you will experience a 1-2% increase in your CR.

Other tactics include showing how many sales a product has made over time, with a stock bar to show how many have already sold or a countdown stock bar to indicate how many items are left in stock. Both are powerful and can increase your CR by another 1-2%.

Creating live movement on the page with timers and bars really gives a sense of urgency to your prospects and moves them along in the process to purchase from you. They think, "I'd better act quickly. There are only a few left, and I don't want to miss out!" It is a sound marketing strategy that works.

In terms of actual conversion rate, aim for 3-10%, depending on the type of deal you're offering.

For example, with the Free Plus Shipping model, expect to be in the 7-10% range which is great, but has a lower profit margin. Retail-priced products typically fall in the 3-5% range. They convert less but have higher margins, so you have to test and see which offer type works best for you in your particular niches.

It might be tempting to start with retail-priced products ($15 or higher), but I highly recommend that you begin your e-commerce business with the Free Plus Shipping model, where the product itself is free, but you charge your customers $9.95 for shipping. It works wonders and is a great way to start learning about Facebook Ads and conversion tactics, and to build up your pixel data. (This will be covered in later chapters.)

You might be surprised how well the Free Plus Shipping model works on your store. It's effective with all types of products and niches, but even more so with jewelry such as necklaces, bracelets, and rings.

Giving away these types of items on Facebook is an event. People love it. They feel they are getting incredible value, and typically share the offers with their friends, which helps increase your conversion rate even further.

Ad targeting depends on how well your store converts. (Targeting is covered later in the book.) You will see how everything ties together, and how each part of the business supports itself like a chain link. If one piece is broken, the whole chain falls apart.

Up Next: In the next chapter, you'll learn how to increase your average order value, bumping up your cart value 2 to 3 times with cutting-edge strategies.

Cash Flow Action Plan

1. Test your store thoroughly on both desktop and mobile devices for ease of use and to ensure everything displays properly and functions correctly.

2. Consider where you can add scarcity to your product pages to increase your conversion rate.

3. Determine several related products for each item to cross-sell your prospects.

4. Test out the Free Plus Shipping model for at least one week. Did you achieve higher conversion rates and more sales during this period?

Chapter 8

INCREASING YOUR AVERAGE ORDER VALUE

Average order value, or AOV, is critical to keep your profit margins high. Your AOV is the average amount people spend per order at your store. The higher the AOV, the more margin you have to scale your ads.

Think about the upsells you see during your everyday routine. You might wake up in the morning and get a Starbucks coffee. As you order, the cashier might ask you whether you want any food or a larger size of coffee. If you've ever said yes, you've just been upsold!

McDonald's is probably most notorious for their upsells. I'm sure you've been asked "Do you want fries with that?" Even at the supermarket, buying is encouraged through enticing deals such as Buy 2, Get 1 Free. Upsells are everywhere. You probably don't even notice them anymore. The next time you go shopping, pay attention to the deals out there intended to raise AOV.

With the Free Plus Shipping model, you can expect an AOV of around $15. With retail-priced products ($20 average selling price), expect an AOV of $25 to $35. Both can work well, but the best method for your store will again depend on your products and niches. Testing will allow you to find the sweet spot between conversion rate and AOV. In the end, the main goal is net profit. Money in and money out.

How can you increase your AOV? There are several ways to do this effectively. The first strategy is to offer upsells during the checkout process. The most effective upsell to offer is the same product or a similar one. So if you sell someone a t-shirt, you could offer them the same design but in a different color, for example.

Other effective types of upsell offers include:

- Buy 2 or more items and get free shipping

- Get a 2nd item for $5 off

- Order 2 or more items and get a free gift (EX: cheap bracelet)

- Buy 2 or 3 items and get the next item added to cart free

These are great examples of how you can drastically increase your AOV for higher profit margins.

As technology improves, the checkout process becomes more effective for increasing AOV. For example, the most powerful time to offer an upsell is via a pop-up offer after your customer purchases (after checkout). With one click of the mouse, the customer can upgrade their order to include more of the same product they just ordered or other similar products, without having to input their credit card details again.

These types of upsells convert between 10-30%, depending on where they're offered in the funnel, before or after checkout. So test out multiple variations of upsells to see what works best for you. You might be surprised which one works best. It's usually not the one you predict. So always test to find the most profitable method.

The goal is to keep your AOV high while maintaining a solid conversion rate. These two elements combined will give you maximum profit on your store and the highest return on investment from your ads.

The next component of the AOV equation is lifetime value (LTV). LTV is the amount a customer spends with you over the course of 12 months (typically). It's good to aim for at least a $100 LTV. There are several ways to obtain this.

For one, you can send out email promotions to your buyers list 2 to 3 times per week offering discounts, coupons, free shipping, and new product lines. This will encourage your customers to return to your store and buy more products, increasing LTV.

You can also run upsell ad campaigns to your buyers list, which is highly effective. (This concept will be covered in a later chapter.) Upsell ad campaigns have big returns on investment and can skyrocket your LTV. Run these promotions in conjunction with your email campaigns to hit your buyers list from all angles and to "bounce" them from platform to platform.

The more interactions your customers get from you on different platforms (email, Facebook, Instagram), the fresher your brand and store will stay in their minds. Also, the more likely they will return to make additional purchases.

This is a great way to "retarget" your customers, because they say it takes 7 times for someone to see your ad before they take action. This number should be lower with your buyers list, but still you get the point.

After a few months of testing, you'll start to gain some clarity about your AOV and LTV. Then you'll know exactly how much you can spend on your ads while still remaining profitable over time.

For example, if you have a $100 LTV, you know you can spend up to $50 to acquire a customer with your ads and still have 100% ROI. Knowing your numbers and doing simple math like this can make all the difference with a store that does $100/day revenue as compared to a store that does $10,000/day.

It all comes down to risk tolerance and understanding your true conversion rate, AOV, and LTV.

Up Next: In the next chapter, you'll learn about Facebook Ads and how wildly powerful they can be. You will explore their ability to laser-target and scale your campaigns. This is where it gets really interesting!

Cash Flow Action Plan

1. What types of upsells can you offer your prospects?

2. What types of email promotions can you send to your buyers list?

3. What types of upsell ad campaigns can you run to encourage customers to make additional purchases at your store?

4. What are your specific CR, AOV, and LTV goals?

Chapter 9

ADVERTISING WITH CONFIDENCE

We are living in a time when it has never been easier to get an online business up and running. Technology has come so far that, within days, you can have your store live and sending tons of affordable traffic to your site. Facebook Ads are the Holy Grail of laser-targeted, scalable traffic.

Before Facebook existed, retailers used to have a much bigger challenge reaching customers.

To determine what products to sell and whether customers would buy them, they would have to research as much as possible and then stock up on inventory based on their best guesses.

Also, they'd have to build and maintain a brick and mortar location. That meant rent, upkeep, bills, and staff. Even the location of a store could result in success or failure.

The traffic source would be controlled by whomever happened to drive or walk past the store, or by the ads placed in newspapers or magazines. Larger businesses might have paid for advertising on television or a billboard. The targeting was much more difficult. How could they know that the right people were seeing their ads?

Even today, some dinosaur retailers use these old-fashioned methods, but they are dying out. If you keep an eye on big box retailers, you'll notice they're not nearly as successful as they once were. Extremely well-known brand stores are closing down, unable to keep up with online marketing.

As more and more people discover the power of Facebook advertising and more customers shop online, the faster profits of these over-leveraged companies will fall.

Some stores that have restructured or closed down completely include: Aeropostale, American Apparel, Wal-Mart, and Future Shop.

The smart brands focus more on their online presence. With giants such as Amazon, eBay, and Etsy paving the way for customers to experience the convenience of purchasing online, this shopping method is becoming more and more common. If you don't have an online shop, you're missing out on huge profits.

Once you start exploring the potential of Facebook Ads, you might be shocked by how much data is collected on each person. Statistics about how much a person earns or what kind of car they drive. It's actually quite astounding how much personal information has been collected. For advertising, it's a gold mine of helpful details.

Once you master Facebook Ads, you'll never have to go anywhere else for advertising. The potential reach is incredible. You can conceivably spend tens of thousands of dollars per day with Facebook Ads and still have plenty of room to scale your campaigns.

Combine this massive ability to scale with the most advanced targeting out there and you have the greatest ad platform online. The best part is that you can run ads with any budget. Whether you start with $5 per day or $500, it's up to you. You will see results either way.

To truly understand the power of Facebook Ads, you must understand the campaign structure and learn how to set up your ads for success. Ideally, set up one campaign per product in your store. This will allow you to clearly see where you're getting traction. It will also allow Facebook to determine which audience segment to target based on where conversions are coming from. (More on this later.)

Inside each campaign, you can create as many ad sets as you want. You will eventually have hundreds of ad sets testing many different variables of targeting and ad types. Ad sets allow you to select your audience, choose your optimization type, and indicate what you are willing to bid on the traffic you're buying.

The advertisements themselves go inside the ad sets. You typically only want 1 ad per ad set, unless you are split testing 2 different types of ads (EX: image and copy).

It is good practice to always launch at least 2 duplicate ads inside the same ad set, because Facebook will always favor one ad over the other, even if they are exactly the same, due to different targeted audiences. Because one ad will perform better than the other, you can then simply pause the underperforming (bad) one. Most marketers don't apply this method, so use this to your advantage to create winning ads with ease.

We use three types of campaigns most often: Website Conversion (WC), Clicks to Website (CTW), and Page Post Engagement (PPE). Approximately 90% of our campaigns are WC. These are by far the best-performing campaigns so I recommend sticking with WC in the start to get your feet wet. Sometimes we use CTW and PPE campaigns to scale out. (This will be covered in Chapter 12.)

WC campaigns use the Facebook pixel for optimization. This pixel is a small 1px by 1px image that loads onto your store's Thank You page after a purchase is made. The pixel stores all the data about your buyers and tells Facebook which people to show your ads to for the most conversions (sales). This tactic is incredibly effective and is responsible for the success of multiple 7-figure stores.

The Ad Set field on Facebook is where you select your target audience. The most common audiences we target in our business are precise interests, broad interests, flex audiences, lookalike audiences, and custom audiences.

When you first test a new product, always begin with the most targeted type of audience, precise interests. Precise interests are the lowercase words that identify affiliations such as associations, clubs, hobbies, magazines, pages, and websites. This is where you'll get the fastest traction with a new product and discover whether it's going to sell or not.

You should have an audience size around 200,000-500,000 for this one. With these types of ads, start your budget at $5 per day per ad set.

Figure 9.1 Precise interests (Facebook Ads)

Broad interests is the next type of targeting to test. They are capitalized words such as "Fishing Reel" (as opposed to precise, which would be lowercase "fishing reel"). These types of interests should only be targeted after you've properly vetted the product with precise interests and you know it's selling well. The audience size for this type should be 1-2 million and the price set at $25 per day per ad set.

Flex audiences use the power of intersecting multiple layers of interests. This is also known as narrowing

Detailed Targeting ⓘ INCLUDE people who match at least ONE of the following ⓘ

Interests > Additional Interests

Fishing rod

Fishing tackle

Add demographics, interests or behaviors | **Suggestions** | **Browse**

Exclude People or Narrow Audience

Figure 9.2 Broad interests (Facebook Ads)

your audience, because you can target people who have particular interests. An example would be an outdoor business targeting people who like fishing, hunting, and hiking. These would likely be avid outdoorsmen and women who would be more likely to convert into sales with your products because they are die-hard fans of the niche.

Detailed Targeting ⓘ INCLUDE people who match at least ONE of the following ⓘ

Interests > Additional Interests

Fishing rod

Fishing tackle

Add demographics, interests or behaviors | **Suggestions** | **Browse**

and MUST ALSO match at least ONE of the following ⓘ   ✕

Interests > Additional Interests

deepsea fishing

Add demographics, interests or behaviors | **Suggestions** | **Browse**

Figure 9.3 Flex targeting (Facebook Ads)

Lookalike audiences (LLAs) are quite powerful and scalable, as they are typically between 2-10 million in audience size and are created from valuable data. The more people in the audience, the larger budget it will support.

LLAs are audiences you create from custom audiences (CAs). CAs are created from people who visit your product page. You typically want 1,000 or more people in your CA before you create an LLA from it. You can create between 1-10% of your LLAs from your CAs. I like to test all 10 of them, because you never know what's going to work.

Start with a budget of $50 per day per ad set with LLAs to reap the full rewards, as Facebook needs more data on a daily basis to optimize these beasts.

Figure 9.4 Lookalike targeting (Facebook Ads)

Finally, custom audiences are people who reach your product page. Use these audiences to build out LLAs but also to retarget your prospects. Retargeting is highly profitable and produces the highest return on your investment by far. You will see 4x-5x revenue per ad spend on average.

It's best practice to include ads that offer different color options of the product you want customers to buy. They might not be interested in a silver necklace, but they might instead buy a gold one.

The primary types of advertising posts we suggest you use include:

- Carousel

- Image

- Link

- Right-side

- Video

Approximately 90% of your ads will be photos, or image posts, which are 1200x1200-pixel square images. Use a white background and no text with these ad types to show off your product with a clean format so it appears that someone shared the post instead of having it look like an obvious ad.

This type of ad works best because it takes up a large amount of real estate in the Facebook Newsfeed and gets the most engagement (Likes, Shares, Comments) of any ad types. You can get quite a bit of free viral traffic from these image posts, which is why we like them so much.

The only drawback here is that the image is not clickable. When your prospects click the image, it opens up the posts and they have to click the link inside the description to get to your product page.

Figure 9.5 1200x1200 image ad post

Link post ads are a great way to scale out, because each ad type will reach a different segment of the audiences you're trying to target. This way, you will access different people and maximize the reach of your campaigns.

Link posts are 1200x628, a rectangle. But the big difference is that they're clickable. If someone clicks on the image, they are taken directly to the product page. Link posts work well to drive clicks quickly to your store; however, don't expect them to have the same conversion rate as image posts.

Figure 9.6 1200x628 link ad post

Video posts are one of the cheapest and most affordable ways to get immediate reach with your ads. They don't always convert, but when they do, it's huge.

The video itself is not clickable to your product page, but the headline is. After the video is done playing, a button to visit your product page appears as well. The best types of videos to test are customer testimonials and product demonstrations. Slide shows can also work well. Once again, it's all about testing to see which video gets you the most sales.

Figure 9.7 1280x720 video ad post

Carousel ads display multiple images horizontally using a scroll-type feature. These are mostly used to retarget your custom audience, but can also be used with normal traffic campaigns.

They are highly effective and, at the time this book was written, still fairly new to the Facebook Ads platform. Because many people haven't seen them before, they're considered new creative, which gets higher click-through rates and conversions than normal link post ads. The images here are clickable to your product page, which is a nice bonus.

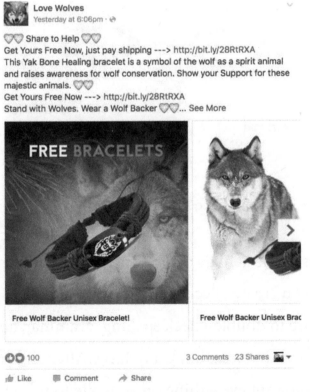

Figure 9.8 Carousel ad post

Finally, right-side ads are (not surprisingly) located on the right side of the Facebook Newsfeed. Smaller in size and clickable image, these ads are truly hit or miss.

They only work with desktop traffic; no mobile option here. So if you find that you're getting good conversion with desktop traffic, test their performance, as they are highly scalable.

SPONSORED   Create Ad

Northskull
northskull.com
Shop bracelets, cuffs, necklaces, rings, cufflinks and cardholders.

Figure 9.9 Right-side ad post

In terms of the actual content, there are many resources to help you create effective, innovative ads. Also, make sure to double-check spelling, grammar, and punctuation before adding anything. After all your hard work, you want everything on your site to reflect your brand professionally. You might even consider hiring a professional copy editor, who can ensure your content is clear, accurate, and engaging.

You can choose many ways to mix and match ad campaigns, ad sets, and ad types. It's all about testing with Facebook Ads, so you have to get out there and keep launching ads to see what works best with the products in your store.

Up Next: Next, you'll learn more about targeting and how to find highly profitable audiences who will buy your products.

Cash Flow Action Plan

1. When will you use precise interests for your Facebook Ads?

2. How could lookalike audiences benefit your product cross-selling?

3. What are the advantages and disadvantages of different ad posts? Which ones will you try for your online business?

4. Draft a sample campaign using the options in this chapter, including a variety of ad sets and ad types.

Chapter 10

TARGETING FOR RESULTS

This is one of the most important concepts in marketing. It's key that you pay attention, take notes, and re-read this chapter a few times. Targeting effectively can be the difference between losing money or making it with your campaigns, so listen up!

You can target your audiences many different ways with Facebook Ads. But you're looking to target buyers. People you know will be interested in buying your products. Doesn't it make sense to show your ads only to those who are most passionate about your products?

It's actually a bit of psychology. You have to reach into the minds of the super passionate and understand their interests. What do these people Like on Facebook?

For example, I love DJing and house music. I have Liked products and software that are relevant to producing music. So that gives you an idea about how to target me.

When searching for your passionate customers, consider magazines and associations they might belong to. These are precise interests.

The best way to start all your campaigns when it comes to targeting is to use precise interests. Your ads will display to laser-targeted people first, those who are most likely to buy them, so they will determine whether your products will sell.

These types of precise interest audiences tend to be on the smaller side, around 200,000-1 million. You will need to group several precise interests together to reach a decent audience size. I recommend aiming for a 300k audience size to start.

Remember, precise interests use lowercase such as "nursing" as opposed to broad interests, which begin with capital letters and usually have audiences in the millions.

There are two essential steps to finding profitable precise interests to test with your campaigns.

The first step is to use Audience Insights, which is a tool inside your Facebook Ads account. It allows you to search country, age, gender, and keywords (interests).

First type in a broad interest keyword such as "Fishing", then click on the Page Likes tab.

Figure 10.1 Audience Insights (Facebook)

The following illustration shows a list of Facebook Page Likes for people who Like the "Fishing" interest (keyword). If you click on the Affinity column, it will sort from highest to lowest. Affinity shows you the audiences most targeted and likely to buy. You are trying to find 15x or greater affinity interests here.

Page Likes
Facebook Pages that are likely to be relevant to your audience based on Facebook Page likes.

Page	Relevance ⓘ	Audience	Facebook	Affinity ⓘ	▾
Abu Garcia	13	396.1K	440.7K	4.2x	
GetZone Hunting	22	347.5K	387.5K	4.2x	
Berkley Fishing	4	552K	623K	4.2x	
Apple Creek Whitetails Ranch	3	675.6K	858.8K	3.7x	
SA Fishing	49	336.7K	430.1K	3.7x	
Ugly Stik	1	751.5K	1,000K	3.5x	
BASS	47	383.9K	513.8K	3.5x	
Deer & Deer Hunting	52	356.3K	486K	3.5x	
Drury Outdoors	50	367.4K	511.6K	3.4x	
Mystik Lubricants	62	348.9K	491.2K	3.3x	

See More

Figure 10.2 Page Likes (sorted by affinity)

Start making lists of interests with high affinity. You can then plug them into the Interests box one by one and find even more high affinity interests. This method allows you to quickly find 50-100 precise interests. Now use these interests with your ads to test different audiences and see where you get traction.

You can repeat this process for broad interests as well (such as "Fishing"). However, because these include huge audiences of people who might not be as passionate or relevant to your product, it's best to intersect. As mentioned in the previous chapter, this was part of my flex method.

Intersecting is where you have someone who Likes two pages that are about the same topic, for example "Fishing" and "Fishing Rod". You can intersect broad interests with broad, or broad with precise, or even precise with precise. Keep in mind that your audience size will decrease, but you can intersect many combinations of different interests to tap into targeted audiences who haven't seen your ad.

Testing is vital here. Launch several $5-$25 budget ads to see what works best for you, then you can scale up and out. (You will learn about this in another chapter.)

For a new product, you should test at least 5-10 different types of audiences before giving up. You'll already know that these products sell, because they've been proven on the Facebook Newsfeed with other advertisers' posts that have high engagement (Likes, Comments, Shares).

The next step in finding interests is to visit Google.com and search for topics such as niche associations, websites, magazines or products. The goal is to uncover interests you didn't find using the Audience Insights method. This is highly effective for discovering valuable interests that other marketers didn't pursue.

Start with around a 300k audience size for your first set of ads. Then if those work, you can start testing larger audiences (1mm-2mm) and from there test even larger ones (2mm-10mm). Don't shy away from larger audiences and bigger budgets, as these types of ads can bring in significant revenue for your store.

In terms of organizing your ad sets for testing different audiences, you should group similar types of interests together. Association interests would be one ad set, websites would be another, and magazines yet another. This way you can identify which type of audience converts best for your product in your given niche.

You might be surprised what actually works when you test all these different audience types. It's usually not the audience you expect to yield the best results, so test thoroughly and find those winners!

For a more advanced tactic, read your competitors' posts, click on the Comments, and find specific people who said they purchased the product. Then review their Likes.

Compare 10-20 buyers' Likes (interests) and watch for any similar ones that you could potentially target with your ads. This works great to find hidden buyer interests that no one else is targeting. It will also help you gain a deeper understanding of your niche.

Up Next: In the next chapter, you will learn about reporting inside Facebook Ads and how to optimize your campaigns for profitability.

Cash Flow Action Plan

1. Identify 10 precise interests for one of your niches.

2. Find 20 broad interests for one of your niches.

3. Research 10 buyer interests from a competitor's post for one of your niches.

4. Determine 5 associations, 5 websites, and 5 magazines for one of your niches using Google search.

Chapter 11

REPORTING THE FACTS

Imagine you're driving to a local baseball game, but you have no idea how to get there. I call this "flying blind" and it's the worst possible way to operate your e-commerce business.

You might think this is common sense, but you'd be surprised how many students I've coached who have admitted they don't track their profits. Instead, they just look at the numbers on Facebook reports without actually correlating their revenue in Shopify minus their spend in Facebook.

Facebook doesn't actually record data accurately. It gives you a rough idea of how well ads are doing, but if you actually crunched the numbers, you'd see a pretty big discrepancy.

Therefore it's critical that you track your ads daily and in detail to find where you might be wasting your ad spend. The ultimate goal is to cut ads that aren't profitable.

After pausing all these negative ROI ads, you will be left with profitable ads that work. Focus on your winning ads, and find out exactly who is buying. That's the beauty of the Facebook Ads Reporting feature. You can see where you're getting the most traction and focus your ad spend on those hot spots.

Inside the Facebook Ads Manager, under Measure & Report, Ads Reporting, you will see a default report. Customize the columns to display only vital data you'll need to optimize your campaigns.

From left to right, display the data as follows:

- CPM (cost per mille, or thousand, impressions)
- CTR (click-through rate)
- CPC (cost per click)
- Budget
- Amount Spent
- Purchase Conversion Value
- Cost Per Purchase
- Purchases

Note: Make sure you're viewing Ad Sets and not Campaigns or Ads. This is the report you will review several times daily to manage, optimize, and scale your ads.

CTR..	Fre...	CPM (...	CPC (...	Bid	Budget	Amoun...	Purchas...	Purchas...	Cost p..
5.15%	1.28	$2.75	$0.59	Auto Impression...	$100.00 Daily	$574.26	$1,936.20	18	$31.90
5.15%	1.08	$5.80	$0.85	Auto Impression...	$100.00 Daily	$555.76	$4,860.06	38	$14.63
3.62%	1.40	$5.57	$0.75	Auto Impression...	$75.00 Daily	$480.22	$1,801.73	31	$15.49
4.39%	1.13	$7.53	$0.67	Auto Impression...	$75.00 Daily	$431.66	$2,726.90	28	$15.42
3.89%	1.23	$3.30	$0.39	Auto Impression...	$75.00 Daily	$431.43	$3,029.44	25	$17.26
5.10%	1.08	$11.39	$0.74	Auto Impression...	$50.00 Daily	$318.39	$2,901.22	26	$12.25
3.24%	1.06	$7.91	$1.09	Auto Impression...	$75.00 Daily	$302.41	$1,518.10	18	$16.80
4.02% Per Imp...	1.50 Per Per...	$6.84 Per 1,000 ...	$0.81 Per Action			$24,334.33 Total Spent	$153,714.77 Total	1,464 Total	$16.62 Per Action

Figure 11.1 Reporting (Facebook Ads Manager)

So what should you look for in terms of ad performance? Number one, your CPC should be around $1.00 or less. We find this CPC is most profitable with many types of ads, especially 1200x1200 image posts. CPM should be $10 or less. CTR isn't a huge concern, but anything more than 2.5% is good.

The most important metric is money in and money out. How much did you spend and how much did you make? Look at your ad spend for the ad set then your Purchase Conversion Value. Aim for a conversion value 2x-3x or greater compared to your ad spend. This will get you in the 50-100% ROI range, which is scalable.

Next, dive into the demographics and see who is buying. Age, gender, placement, and device are the most common areas to look at. If I see certain segments doing extremely well, I will duplicate the ad several times with each different segment per ad and see if I can get an ROI boost.

You might be shocked at the difference in ROI between iPhones and Android phones, for example. You might be even more impressed with Samsung phones; they convert really well.

65+	Female	13	0.26%	4.67	$4.74	$1.82
45–54	Female	16	0.15%	3.86	$4.31	$2.38
55–64	Male	—	—	4.40	$4.67	—
55–64	Female	14	0.16%	4.63	$4.10	$2.52
65+	Male	—	—	3.39	$5.01	—
25–34	Female	4	0.09%	2.97	$3.90	$4.51
35–44	Female	8	0.11%	3.48	$4.04	$3.27
18–24	Female	1	0.05%	2.85	$3.45	$7.43
35–44	Male	1	0.17%	4.48	$4.31	$2.55

Figure 11.2 Demographic breakdown (Facebook Ads Manager)

Breaking out the demographic segments of your audience is a great way to scale out. The more ads you launch, the more you spend, and the more you should profit if you're cutting them fast enough.

So focus on launching 5-10 ads per day and aim to have at

least 50 ads running at all times (100-200 ads are better).

When should you cut your ads? If you're just starting out, use $5 budgets and run the ad for 3 days minimum before cutting if no sale occurs. The budget is so low that Facebook needs more time to optimize it for you and find the buyers.

Starting with a bigger budget such as $25 or $50 is even better. At this amount, I would run the ad for 1-2 days before cutting if no sales.

Overall, you should monitor your ads carefully. Check reports every 3-4 hours to confirm that your ads are performing well. If they're not performing, simply pause them and restart tomorrow to give them another go. Ads can be random when it comes to performance, so you have to throw mud on the wall and see what sticks.

When you have three duplicate ads in an ad set, one of them will always perform better than the other two. Pause the two bad ads and continue with the remaining ad. It's amazing how much difference you will see between the three ads in terms of CTR, CPC, and Cost Per Purchase.

The most critical takeaway from this chapter is this: know your numbers! It blows my mind how many store owners don't bother tracking their daily spend, revenue, profit, or ROI.

If you don't know the health of your business, how can you expect to grow it? Use a simple spreadsheet to track your numbers daily. The idea is to grow steadily, week after week and month after month.

Up Next: Ready to start scaling up your ads? In the next chapter, you will learn how to go from $100/day to $1,000/day profit.

Cash Flow Action Plan

1. Set up a simple spreadsheet to track your daily profit and loss.

2. Set up custom reporting in Facebook Ads Manager to track your ads for optimization.

3. Which 10-year age groups could you break out into additional ads?

4. Determine how and when you will monitor your ads daily to ensure optimal performance.

114

Chapter 12

SCALING YOUR AUDIENCES

Now comes the most exciting part of the entire business model. The time when you take your best-performing ads and scale them for big profits. Two main ways to scale are up and out. Scaling up is easier, but requires a larger budget. Scaling out with smaller budgets is recommended if you're just starting out.

SCALING UP

The best way to scale up is to simply increase the budgets on your best-performing ads. Be careful not to raise them too high too quickly, or it will alter Facebook's algorithm, causing your costs to skyrocket. A good rule of thumb is to increase your budget on each best-performing ad by 25% per day maximum. You could also choose to only scale up your budgets every 2 days. Test your campaigns to see what works best.

An example would be starting with a $25 budget that produces $50 in revenue. The next day, you would increase the budget by $5 to $30.

It's best practice to scale up budgets in the early morning, before 9am in your ad account time zone. This will give Facebook a full day to re-optimize with your new budget.

Keep scaling up your budgets by 25% every day or every other day, until you reach the ceiling where your ROI starts to drop enough so it's no longer profitable. At this stage, start walking your budgets back down, using the same 25% rule until you are profitable again. In this way, you will find the sweet spot between volume of sales and ROI.

To scale out, duplicate your best performers. Start by duplicating 2-3 ads per day from the exact same ad set. After you duplicate the ad set 10 times or so, you'll notice some duplicates will work and some will not, just like with regular ads.

On average, you should be able to find at least 3-5 duplicate ad sets that perform well. Use the same 25% rule for scaling budgets on these duplicated ad sets.

Another method of scaling out is used to increase your reach, ad spend, and profit even further. Break out your ad sets into different segments of demographics and placements. Age, gender, and mobile device are some great examples to use.

Break out the best-performing segments for age groups in 5- or 10-year gaps. For example, 25-34 or 55-59. Gender will be an obvious factor as well, depending on the type of product you are promoting. Placement or mobile devices are useful for breaking out into additional ad sets as well. You will find some products and niches do much better with iPhone users as compared to those with Android phones.

A final way of scaling out is by using other campaign objectives. It's best to use the website conversion objective for 90% of your campaigns. When you're ready to scale out to the furthest extent, try Clicks to Website and PPE campaign objectives to reach different sets of people in your target audiences.

All these forms of scaling will take your campaigns to the next level. They will give you the ability to increase your overall ad spend, which in turn should mean more profits.

At first, you might be concerned about budget and spending too much on Facebook Ads, but if you can view it objectively and look at the cold hard data, you will succeed.

Our biggest enemies when it comes to Facebook Ads and scaling are ourselves. We sometimes hold ourselves back from giving ads enough of a chance to optimize and convert. You need to let an ad run for at least 24 hours to properly optimize.

That being said, when you're starting out, it's best to pause any ads that don't convert into sales around $15-$20. Keep it simple and pause ads aggressively in the start.

If any ads are breaking even, let them run and Facebook will work to optimize them for you. The big winners should have their budgets scaled up daily and broken out into segmented ads.

There is one more helpful method for scaling. Different

types of people in your audiences react to images differently. So to scale even further, try split testing different images of your product with your ads.

In addition to the standard white background with a clean product image, you could try using an image of a real person wearing the product, or do an Instagram-style image where the product is set on a table with other items, giving it a luxury appeal.

Up Next: The next chapter will add additional sales and revenue to your store automatically. It's a special type of ad that will run forever and continue to be profitable for as long as traffic is being sent to your store.

Cash Flow Action Plan

1. If you have a $60 budget that is performing with 100% ROI, or 2x your ad spend, what would you increase it to the next day?

2. If you have maxed out your budget for an ad set, what is the next best step to take when scaling it out?

3. How will you scale out to different segments of your audience using demographics?

4. What other types of campaign objectives will you run after you have maxed out website conversion ads for your products?

Chapter 13

RETARGETING YOUR PROSPECTS

Retargeting ads are the most profitable type you will run with your store. On days when regular ads struggle, retargeting ads will save the day. They consistently give you 4x-10x your ad spend, which equates to 400%-1,000% ROI. If you aren't running these types of ads with your store, you are missing out.

The best part is that after you set them up, they run on autopilot for as long as your store receives traffic. That's because they're targeting people who visited your store but didn't buy, or people who Added to Cart but didn't buy.

As I mentioned earlier, it takes 7 times for someone to see an ad before they take action. Online, I think this number might be lower, but either way retargeting ads are extremely powerful.

Imagine you visited an online store and looked around but didn't make a purchase. Then the next day, you see

another ad for the product you were looking at that entices you to click on it. This time you actually purchase the item.

The reason this works is because life sometimes gets in the way, and people get sidetracked because they're too busy with tasks such as work, their kids, or dinner. But when they get a second chance to purchase your product, it works like a charm.

You can retarget your prospects in several ways. I find the best method is to use ads that read something like this:

"We noticed you added an item to the cart, but didn't complete your purchase. We know that life sometimes gets in the way, so here's a 20% coupon for you to hurry back and buy it now! But don't delay, because the discount won't be around for much longer..."

You could even try additional images or different angles of the product to show them a variety of styles and colors. You never know what will make them return to the store and buy! Split test different variations of your retargeting ads to see what works best.

In terms of placement, we find that mobile newsfeed and right-side perform the best. Again, split test and see what works best for your campaigns. With these types of ads, you can't scale them up or out. You only really need one ad for each type of retargeting you find works best.

The amount you'll be able to scale up the budgets directly correlates to how much fresh traffic you're sending to your store. So the key is to consistently increase the ad spend on your account so that more and more traffic is being sent to your store each day. This will increase your website visitors audience and will essentially feed your retargeting ads to perform for you on autopilot.

Your average cost per sale will be much lower than normal compared to regular ads. Don't be surprised to see half the cost for retargeting ads when you run them.

We notice that our customers actually spend more when they come from a retargeting ad as well. I believe this is due to branding and really making an imprint in our customers' minds.

They're so distracted by other ads and marketers' messages that it's challenging to keep your brand in the forefront of their minds. That's where retargeting helps boost your overall sales and revenue.

On days where you are breaking even or losing money, retargeting will keep you profitable. It's essential you run these ads side-by-side with your regular ads. You never know when you will need them most and they are always profitable.

It's pretty much "set and forget" with retargeting, so create these for your store as soon as possible and watch how well they perform.

Finally, why not try retargeting your current customers with different products? This works extremely well and is a great way to introduce your new products into the marketplace to see whether they'll sell, because your best customers are your current ones. Test this out and see how well it works for you!

Up Next: Want to discover the best way to easily add 15%-30% more revenue to your store? Then read on!

Cash Flow Action Plan

1. Establish a process where you continuously send new traffic to your site in order to make best use of your retargeting efforts.

2. Determine 3-4 different options for retargeting customers who visited your store but didn't make purchases.

3. It takes _____ times for someone to see an ad before they take action. How does this impact your business tactics?

4. Plan how you will entice your current customers to return to your store and buy more.

Chapter 14

REENGAGING YOUR LEADS

This is an area that many store owners don't bother to act on. However, it's a strategy that can instantly boost your sales and save campaigns from losing money. It's called reengaging, and it's a way to speak directly to your potential customers.

When you run 1200x1200 image post ads, you tend to receive a high number of Likes, Shares, and Comments. To reengage, simply respond to people who have commented.

Every comment that comes in should have a personal reply from your team. Also, insert a link at the end of your comment returning them to the product page you're promoting.

This technique works incredibly well, as people realize that you are a real person who is answering their questions and concerns. It also helps with social proof, as others see people interacting with you.

Some people might post unflattering things such as "This store is a scam" or "What a rip-off!". Don't worry, you can simply delete those negative comments and ban those who are trolling your post. Remember you can't please everyone, so try to have thick skin and moderate messages daily. Your goal is to have clean, upbeat, and positive comments on all your ad posts.

To encourage more people to comment so you can reengage them with a link to buy, try asking people to do so within the post itself. You could say something such as, "Comment YES below if you like this!". This increases action on your post, which actually helps drive down traffic costs while giving you a social proof bump.

You should reply to comments with a personal touch, mentioning the person's name and making each reply unique. But eventually you should outsource this task, as it requires a significant amount of time.

Your time is best spent elsewhere such as launching, optimizing, and scaling your ads. At the same time, this reengagement strategy should not be neglected because it's easy money and drives extra traffic and sales to your store on a daily basis.

Figure 14.1 Replying to comments (reengaging)

You might be shocked when some people comment on your ads asking for the link to buy. Even in this day and age, some people have a hard time navigating Facebook or online, in general.

Reengaging acts as a form of retargeting, reminding your prospects to return to your store to buy if they didn't the first time. It's just one more way to interact with your prospects, because you never know how many times they'll need to be reminded before they finally take action and buy one of your awesome products!

Another method that sometimes works well is to run an ad with no link. Show the product as usual (image with a white background), but in the description include something like, "Do you want this? If you do, comment I WANT IT below and we'll show you how to get it!"

It's simple but effective, and you will likely be surprised by how many people comment. Of course, because there's no link in the description, you'll want to use the reengaging strategy to reply to all of these comments with a link to your store. Test it out and see how it works for you.

Don't be like all the other marketers out there. Put in the time with this strategy and watch how much extra profit comes in. It's a powerful method I've used over the years to stabilize our store revenue.

Up Next: In the next chapter, we will cover a topic that is not as sexy, but is absolutely critical to keeping your business afloat and your customers happy.

Cash Flow Action Plan

1. What will you do when someone posts a negative comment on your ad?

2. What are some promotions you can offer people who have commented on your post?

3. How can you weave in storytelling when you reply to people's comments?

4. Schedule a time each day to reply to every comment on every single post.

Chapter 15

FULFILLING YOUR ORDERS

Now that sales are rolling in, it's time to get your product into the hands of your customers. The faster you get it to them, the happier they will be. This chapter will touch on a few select fulfillment options. Ultimately, you will decide which one to use based on your projected margin and customer happiness ratio.

Figure 15.1 AliExpress.com fulfillment

AliExpress is an excellent source for vendors who can fulfill your products. By inputting a customer's details and shipping address into AliExpress, your vendor can ship the goods directly to your customer. This is called drop shipping, and is the most common method in the industry, especially for people just starting an e-commerce business.

There is little to no risk using the drop ship method because you don't have to put up capital for inventory before you start selling products. I highly recommend this method of fulfillment until you get a few months of solid sales under your belt and truly start to understand your niches and products that sell best.

AliExpress has several shipping options. My favorite is ePacket, which costs around $2-$3 and takes 2 weeks on average to arrive at your customer's door. The next best option is Small Packet, but these orders take 2 to 3 weeks to arrive. Small Packet is usually free or only $1, so it gives you a bit more margin to play with. However, my advice is to use ePacket, as 2 weeks is the longest people are typically willing to wait for orders to arrive.

Also, remember to allow for processing time. This is the

time between you ordering the product from your vendor and the item being shipped out. Acceptable processing time is between 2 to 3 days, but I've experienced vendors falling behind on orders. For example, at busy times such as the holidays, vendors can get quite behind and overwhelmed.

This is why tracking numbers are essential. Not only can they reassure a buyer that their product is on its way, it also reassures you that the order is being fulfilled.

Consider hiring a virtual assistant (VA) to handle all your fulfillment if you use the drop shipping method. This person should be able to handle 50 orders per hour with AliExpress. If they process any fewer than this, consider finding someone else who is more efficient.

It's also good practice to input the vendor's tracking numbers into Shopify orders, as this can help improve your store conversion rate. Because our company mainly uses Shopify Payments (Stripe), several different banks actually process our customers' credit cards, and some will not process if you don't provide tracking numbers. When this occurs, the payment will be declined. In addition to losing a sale, the customer may be upset or even complain. Ultimately, this leads to lower conversion rates.

Another option is to use a fulfillment house in the US and actually stock inventory for your best-selling products. This requires capital up front and is considered riskier because you will be stuck with any excess inventory that doesn't sell. This type of fulfillment is reserved for experienced business owners, but when implemented correctly can give your store conversion rate a significant boost.

We have seen double and sometimes triple the purchase conversion rate when we switched to 3-7 day fulfillment from the US. We used this as a strategic promo on our ads and product pages and it worked like a charm.

People these days are so used to getting their products within a few days because of Amazon.com. Their site has conditioned us to expect speedy delivery times combined with bargain pricing.

Eventually, you will get to the US fulfillment stage and it will help significantly to scale your business. Even just a 1% conversion rate bump on your store can really drive up your profitability. Your customers will be happier and most importantly, if you give them a good experience, they'll come back for more.

Lifetime customer value (LTV) is a critical metric to track over a 12-month period. How much is each customer spending on average? Once you know this number, you can start to scale up your ad spend with more Facebook Ad campaigns, because your allowable cost per sale will be much higher.

For example, if you know your average customer is worth $100 within a 12-month period, you can spend up to $50 cost per sale and still attain a 100% ROI.

Do not let your guard down when it comes to fulfillment. It's a crucial part of the business. When I first started working with e-commerce years ago, we lost thousands of dollars in chargebacks and refunds because customers didn't get their orders fast enough.

Stay on top of fulfillment and make sure your vendors are getting the orders out the door.

Up Next: In the next chapter, you'll learn how to handle angry customers and keep them shopping with you for life.

Cash Flow Action Plan

1. Are you going to drop ship or fulfill from the US?

2. Which shipping option will you use: ePacket or Small Packet?

3. Calculate your average LTV per customer.

4. How can you improve shipping times to keep your customers happy?

Chapter 16

COMMUNICATING WITH YOUR CUSTOMERS

How do you calm down an angry customer? How do you deal with chargebacks or refund requests? How do you add a personal touch to your customer service emails so people are treated in a professional manner?

Customers can be demanding at times. In any retail business, you will encounter angry people who want their orders immediately, perhaps because they assume everyone operates the same as Amazon. Make sure you clearly mention shipping times in your order

confirmation email from Shopify. You are essentially a small fish looking to enter a marketplace filled with whales.

This is where personal touch becomes important. Your customer service replies should be firm but empathetic.

For example, if a customer requests a refund because they haven't received their order yet after 1 week when they're saying it's been 3 weeks, it's a simple misunderstanding. It's important to obtain tracking numbers so you can confirm exactly when orders were placed and where packages are in the mail system.

Strive to handle your customers with professionalism and class. Remain calm and objective in your responses. Instead, try apologizing for the shipping delays or offering discount coupon codes for their next purchase. This works well to calm them down and keep them happy. It also encourages them to return to your store and make additional purchases!

For example, our store received an email from a lady who wrote:

> "I just want my necklace that I bought from you. Please send it to me. I like your products. The

creativity is great, but it's a little bit frustrating to continue to get notices about products when I am told there is a delay in getting my order. If you have so many bracelets in stock and ready to be bought, then send my bracelet. I will be more grateful and more likely to recommend to others who have Liked you on Facebook".

My customer service representative responded:

"Hi Janet, thanks for shopping with us. Good news! We have processed your order but we are experiencing a higher than normal shipping time because of all the orders we are receiving. Please allow up to 3 weeks for delivery. We hope you understand. We are doing our best to get your order to you as soon as possible."

Simple replies such as this work well because sometimes people just want to feel heard and acknowledged.

However, some customer situations are more heated. One way to cool off a frustrated or annoyed customer is to offer them discounts on future purchases. We like to offer 20% OFF and sometimes up to 40% OFF if they are really upset. The last thing you want is for people to go online and post bad reviews about your store.

Keeping your customers happy is critical to your success and will save you thousands of dollars in refunds down the road. Take care of your customers properly and they will be loyal for life!

Customer service is the second task you should outsource as soon as possible because it takes quite a bit of time to reply to emails. This service can be outsourced to experienced representatives in the Philippines for $3/hour or less. Many Filipinos have worked for large companies such as Google and AT&T, and are therefore highly experienced and skilled at customer service..

Your time is best spent on launching, optimizing and scaling your Facebook Ad campaigns, not dealing with fulfillment or customers. So outsource these tasks as soon as you are able to.

Up Next: In the next chapter, you'll learn how to remove yourself from the day-to-day operations of your business while still remaining profitable.

Cash Flow Action Plan

1. Determine shipping times for your products and chart for easy reference.

2. Draft email templates for your top 5 most likely customer concerns.

3. Learn more about handling difficult customers in a manner that maintains loyalty to your business through online research, blog posts, or other resources.

4. Establish a goal for outsourcing your customer service functions.

Chapter 17

OUTSOURCING YOUR WORK

You have made it a long way on this journey to cash flow for life. By now, you should be making sales and bringing in revenue daily. Your business should be working like a machine. All your systems in place, firing and optimizing for success. Are you ready to step outside your business?

Either you are working in your business or on it. Which is it for you? Which do you want it to be?

Personally, I'd rather be working on my business than inside of it. Focus on the growth of your business month after month so you know you're heading in the right direction for a potential exit in the future. (More about exit strategies later.)

When you work in your business, your time is maxed out. You're doing all the grunt work. Tasks such as researching products to promote, launching Facebook Ad campaigns, fulfilling orders, and handling customer service requests.

This can all be quite overwhelming, and you most likely will spread yourself too thin if you try to handle this all by yourself.

The solution is to hire an experienced and trained team to handle all your day-to-day tasks. As mentioned in the previous chapters, you first want to outsource fulfillment and customer service. This will free up quite a bit of your time so you can focus on growing your business with more ad campaigns.

The third position you should fill is a virtual assistant to manage your Facebook Pages, where all your ad posts will be placed. This VA's job is to reply to every single comment every day, and to drop links for people to click to your store. They will also reply to your fan page inbox messages and ensure they are handled quickly and professionally.

Your fourth position to fill is a VA for email marketing. You could have this VA send 2-3 custom emails per week to your customer list enticing them to return to your site and buy more products.

It's best to use one of these three promotions for your email campaigns: Free Shipping, Buy 2, Get 1 Free, or

20% OFF Entire Store. All promos should have 24-hour windows during which they are valid. This encourages people to take quick action. Ideally, this VA should have graphic design experience and proficiency with Photoshop or Illustrator.

It's important for your team to report in daily with the number of hours they worked and a detailed list of tasks completed, so you can track their performance and verify that everything is getting done.

If you must approach one of your VAs about a productivity or quality issue, it's best to message them privately and not in front of the entire team.

I use Skype group chats to communicate with my team members. This way we can all see what's coming up for the week in terms of goals and tasks to complete. A more formal way to track tasks is to use an online app called Trello.com. Trello allows you to storyboard your goals daily, weekly, and monthly. Each team member gets their own "card" where you can assign tasks for them to complete.

Eventually, you should hire a project manager (PM), who will directly report to you and manage your store's performance. This person will act as a liaison between you and your team, handling team requests and addressing any issues regarding your store or customers. Serious concerns can be escalated to you when necessary. Your PM should also report financial numbers on a daily, weekly, and monthly basis, showing your growth in terms of revenue, expenses, profit, and ROI.

Where is the best place to hire all these people to manage and run your business? We prefer to use Upwork.com (formerly Odesk). It's an easy way to find quality workers overseas. It also gives you the ability to track their hours and work with screenshots, timers, and more. You will find several prospects and be able to hire quality workers within days.

Work with someone perfect for your team

Figure 17.1 Upwork.com home page

Interview at least 5-10 people before choosing one for a full-time position. Always give them a sample task to see how they perform. You will notice how widely different people perform with the same task, allowing you to cherry pick the rock stars. Your whole team should be high quality, because even one bad link in the chain can seriously hurt your business.

Take care of your team and get them the equipment they need to work comfortably from their home or office. Good quality computers, desks, and chairs are great investments in your team and will show them how committed you are.

You want them to feel as if they are truly part of your company and there for the long term. Give them time off when they need it, and surprise them with bonuses if they perform well each quarter.

Up Next: The next chapter will guide you to scale your business even further than you ever thought possible.

Cash Flow Action Plan

1. List the tasks and functions you would like to outsource for your business.

2. Determine whether your budget supports outsourcing. If not, set financial goals to achieve the amount needed.

3. Detail the expectations for each VA position you plan to fill. Include communication preferences, tasks required, time frames, etc.

4. Make a plan for interviewing and hiring your first virtual assistant position.

Chapter 18

FOCUSING ON LIFETIME VALUE

Do you know how much each customer is worth to you? You really should, because this will dictate the amount you're able to spend to acquire each customer. The more lifetime value (LTV) you can get from your customers, the more you can spend on advertising campaigns to get even more new people through the door.

A solid LTV goal is $100. So if you know that a customer is worth $100 over a certain number of months, you should be comfortable spending up to $50 to acquire said customer. This will keep you in line with your 100% ROI goal (double your money). Most small businesses don't think this way so you can use it to your advantage to take over a niche marketplace.

On average, you will spend $5-$10 acquiring each new customer and your competition will be aiming for these amounts as well. However, they will likely pause their campaigns once they reach $15-$20 ad spend with no sale. This is your opportunity to strike, and because you know the LTV of your customers, you can spend more to win. The business that can spend more acquiring customers always comes out on top.

How do you increase LTV with your store? By upselling and cross-selling. You can achieve this with ads targeting people who have already bought from you and by sending weekly emails to your customer list.

Using these two strategies together is so powerful that after 3-6 months, you will start to see your LTV rise. You want people ordering from you at least once per month, so you'll need to run strong monthly promotions to entice them to buy again.

Another way to increase LTV is to increase your average order value (AOV). A Buy 2, Get 1 Free promotion will help increase your AOV and, in turn, also your LTV.

You can also offer upsells before people check out to encourage them to add more items to their carts to increase your AOV and LTV. The idea is to have customers spend more during each shopping session. So tempt them with deals such as a free item when they buy 2 or more, or free shipping when they add 3 or more items to the cart. There are many ways you can use this strategy to get AOV and LTV up.

Consider an iceberg, where 80% of its mass actually lies beneath the water. Customer LTV is similar, in that 80% of the revenue you get from a customer should come in approximately 3-12 months after you acquire them, if you do a good job of increasing their LTV.

Increasing your LTV means you are increasing your profits. It's as simple as that. So you need to make sure you are reaching your customers through multiple channels such as Facebook Ads, email campaigns, Instagram, Pinterest, and Twitter. The more they consider your brand and engage with you, the more they will trust you and return for additional purchases.

Reward your top-spending customers by offering them deep discounts (up to 50%), which will encourage them to spend even more with you. These top spenders are like ambassadors of your brand and will often refer new business to you.

Contact the people who buy most frequently and ask them to join a referral program. You could assign points for each referral or even give 20% OFF to both the original customer and person referred.

You have to get creative here and—you guessed it—testing will be key. Split test a different promotion each month and try to tie it in to events that happen throughout the year. Obvious high-volume periods include Black Friday (the Friday after Thanksgiving in US), Cyber Monday (the Monday after Thanksgiving), winter holidays (Christmas, Hanukkah, Kwanzaa), and Easter.

But you can wrap numerous other events into your promotions to help increase LTV. Put together a promotional calendar for the year and map out which promotions you plan to use and when so you'll be well-prepared.

Finally, a great way to increase your LTV is by offering a continuity, or monthly membership, program. This can really explode the LTV on your store because you start stacking paying members who are rebilled month after month. You can exponentially grow your business this way quickly, but it's highly advanced and not recommended for people just starting out.

With this subscription model, you could offer people

deep discounts for life, as long as they are paying monthly members. You can even send them 1 or 2 free gifts per month as part of a $20/month package, for example.

I hope the wheels are turning here and you are starting to see the power of LTV with your store.

Up Next: In the next chapter, we'll discuss branding and why it's essential for growing your business and lining it up for a 7-figure exit.

Cash Flow Action Plan

1. What types of promotions can you run with your customer base to increase LTV?

2. What is your store's LTV after 3 months? After 6 months? After 12 months?

3. What is the most you can spend to acquire a new customer while maintaining 100% ROI?

4. What could you send your customers monthly to get them on a continuity program?

Chapter 19

BRANDING YOUR BUSINESS

The problem with most business owners and marketers these days is that they don't have any patience. They constantly think about the short-term profits but never want to play the long game. But you need to do both. You need short-term and long-term goals for your business to truly succeed.

One long-term consideration is branding, which is essential to keep your products at the forefront of your customers' minds. In fact, over the next few years I believe there will be a huge shift from a conversion mindset to a branding mindset within the industry and marketplace.

Now is your chance to use this knowledge to your advantage and start working on branding your store immediately.

With the rise in popularity of Snapchat and other social platforms, branding is becoming more important than ever. People want to connect with your brand, store, and image. They don't want to simply be sold to.

So focus on the why, not the what. Show them images that are trending on Instagram or tweet about your latest product styles on Twitter. If you do a model photo shoot with your products, take some extra photos and upload them to your Facebook Fan Page.

The most common and easiest way to brand your store is to include your logo on every piece of content or ad you share. That way, people will start to recognize your logo everywhere they go. It doesn't have to be big or obnoxious. You can place it on the top corner of your images and videos.

You could also approach social media influencers who have large followings and send them one of your products for free. Ask them to review it. Even if they ask for a fee, it will be worth it, because the most powerful type of advertising is referrals.

When they drop your ads on their pages (any social media platform), their followers will show great interest simply because they recommended you. The same strategy has been tested and proven to work repeatedly in the affiliate marketing space.

In order for your store to stand out from the competition in a sea of copycats, you need to have a unique look and feel. Find custom fonts, colors, and images that portray your brand as unique. When people visit your store, they should be wowed, have a fantastic experience, and remember you.

Besides doing photo shoots with professional models wearing your products, you can also shoot interesting video such as 360-degree shots. Consider this awesome product called Arqspin (arqspin.com), a white turntable that you place your product on. It rotates slowly so you can capture video with your iPhone or digital camera.

As people become more and more tech savvy, ad effectiveness takes a hit, so you need to get your branding game up so your store will rise above your competitors.

You should always have branding campaigns running side-by-side with your acquisition campaigns. This will help you build up your assets long-term so investors and business owners are more likely to be interested in taking it over.

Packaging is also key when it comes to branding. You want your customers to have a unique experience when they receive their orders. Whether it's a fancy black bag or a box that protects and displays your product, you need something memorable and branded to showcase your items.

Check out the bigger e-commerce jewelry stores out there. What is their customer experience like? Order some of their products and reverse engineer their emails, packaging, discount cards, or anything else that helps with branding. This can give you great ideas to apply to your own store.

Do not take branding for granted. It's an essential part of the e-commerce business that many storeowners neglect. You might be surprised what happens when your branding efforts start to kick in. Your store conversion rate will start to rise and you'll get significantly more repeat business and referral traffic.

Up Next: Are you ready to get into some advanced marketing tactics with your store? Product funnels are what we'll dive into next!

Cash Flow Action Plan

1. Which social media influencers on Instagram can you approach to represent your brand?

2. Consider organizing a photo shoot with models to give your brand a more real and luxury feel. Think about which items would benefit most from professional photos.

3. Customize your store's look and feel so it's unique using different fonts, colors, and images.

4. What type of custom packaging can you use to enhance your brand? Research costs to determine your best option.

Chapter 20

UPSELLING WITH FUNNELS

If you want to be more profitable with your e-commerce store and really squeeze every drop of LTV and AOV out of your list that you possibly can, then you need to implement funnels. Funnels are extremely powerful for capturing leads, making sales, and upselling continuity or monthly programs. They are the Holy Grail of the online marketing industry, but not for the faint of heart.

You might have heard terms such as lead magnet or trip wires. If not, they are simply giveaways or loss-leader products you can give to your prospects for free to get them in the door.

The Free Plus Shipping business model works perfectly with this. You can break even on the front end by giving away a free necklace, for example, but charging $4.95 for shipping and handling. You will typically see at least a 20% conversion rate here. It's a great way to build a massive buyers list quickly.

After you get a person's name and email, and have identified them as a buyer, you can upsell them to other related products or even a continuity program where they pay monthly.

For example, after they buy the "free" product and just pay shipping, on the Thank You page you could show them 2 or 3 other related products, which they can add to their order with one mouse click.

Unfortunately, one-clicks are not currently possible with Shopify. However, my team is developing a new e-commerce platform that is going to take the industry by storm. It's called Commerce HQ and it will allow you to do one-click upsells and a whole lot more. (More on this later!)

For the time being, you could try ClickFunnels, which is an amazing tool that allows you to build out full product funnels within minutes. It's drag-and-drop, so you can easily build your pages. I highly recommend it. I use it for all my funnels at the moment and they convert really well. I'm able to capture the user's name and email first, then secure them as a buyer with a Free Plus Shipping offer.

Next, I offer them access to a membership area for $19.95/

month where they can cancel at any time. The stick rate for this monthly program is 4-6 months, meaning I'm averaging $80-$120 of revenue per customer who signs up for it. So now I know I can acquire a new customer for $40-$60 and still be highly profitable with 100% ROI.

The membership itself can also be created inside ClickFunnels and you can easily drop in some videos related to your niche that you find online (EX: from YouTube). Call it content curation. Make certain the content is shareable. It's even better to create the videos yourself.

Funnels can be quite profitable. You can use them in conjunction with your Shopify store to add great value to your business. They can instantly boost your LTV and AOV so you're able to spend more on ads and make more profit. They're also a huge asset when it comes to selling your store down the road.

You should track your numbers carefully when you use funnels like this. Cost per click, cost per lead, cost per sale, and cost per signup (monthly program) are important metrics to review. They act as levers for your funnels; by improving them, you will improve your ROI greatly.

You should also set up an email autoresponder that sends out messages daily to persuade prospects to come back and buy if they didn't the first time, or to sign up for the monthly program. You can run retargeting ads to accomplish the same objective.

It's good practice to split test all elements on your funnel pages including headlines, images, copy/text, and emails. One great split-testing platform is VWO, or Visual Website Optimizer (VWO.com), which will automatically split test several elements at the same time.

You will likely find interesting results, because different combinations of split tests work very differently for increasing conversion. This is called multi-variate testing, where you test multiple variations of your pages at the same time. Sometimes we have more than 50 tests running simultaneously, and typically 1 or 2 combinations will come out on top. This process can sometimes double your conversion rate!

Up Next: Want to sell your store to an investor for 7 figures? Then don't miss the next chapter!

Cash Flow Action Plan

1. What related products could you upsell your customers in a funnel?

2. What types of videos could you put in a members area for your core niches?

3. Which email autoresponder will your company use? (ActiveCampaign, MailChimp, AWeber)

4. Which elements can you split test on your funnel pages to increase your conversion rates?

Chapter 21

EXITING FOR 7 FIGURES

This is easily the most exciting chapter in the book, because here you will finally learn how to exit your store and sell it for 7 figures! Wouldn't it be incredible to receive a check with that many zeros on it? It's an enormous influx of cash you can use to fund your next business, buy a house, or simply save for retirement. This is the dream.

So you want to sell your store for $1,000,000? No problem, all you need is 6-12 months of sales data, solid revenue growth, and $35,000/mo in net profit. We use Empire Flippers (EmpireFlippers.com) who charge 15% on the purchase price of the sale of your store. They typically value stores at 30 times your net monthly profit. That's how I came up with $35,000/mo net profit to get a valuation of a million dollars.

So you need to hit $1,167/day net profit to reach your $35,000/mo goal. If you have 6-12 months of profits in this amount, investors will be interested in buying your store for a million cash.

The goal is to show growth month after month and not have any unusual or wild swings. Investors will understand if you have a huge uptick in sales for the fourth quarter because of the holiday season, but the rest of the year should be mostly stable.

The average time frame for selling a store is 3 months (90 days). First, connect with Empire Flippers who will audit your store, your traffic, and of course your sales. If they think it's a good fit and can sell quickly, they will list your business for sale on their site. They will sometimes conduct an audio interview with you as well to help increase the chance of selling it, especially if it's a complicated business model.

To sell your store quickly and for top dollar, you'll need to have 90% of the business outsourced, because the new owner will likely want to be as hands-off as possible. Also the new owner will want you to give them 1-2 months of business support. The best way to deliver training is via screen share videos in which you can walk them through all the systems and processes of the business.

The name of the game is to create an e-commerce store, build it up, and sell it. Then build up another store and sell it as well. There's no limit to how many stores you can build up at the same time to sell 6-12 months down the road. However, I advise building up and selling just one store a time.

Also, when you sell your store, the new owner will most likely want you to sign a 2- or 3-year non-compete agreement. It's typically quite specific and just says you can't run the exact same products on another store. This is why it's best to build up and sell a variety of niche stores.

A niche store typically offers just one key item, for example, FishingShirts.com. With a niche store, you can have multiple products or sometimes just one product that revolves around that niche. I have seen many successful stores that only have one main best-selling product and a few upsell items related to it.

When you are building up a niche store for sale, try to choose a niche that will sell year-round, as investors do not typically like seasonal stores or products. They prefer businesses that can be activated all year round.

An example of a seasonal store would be BBQShirts.com

(not a real website). People usually don't buy barbecue products in the winter, so stores such as this should be avoided at all costs.

Do you have a store you think would fit the requirements to list and potentially sell on Empire Flippers? If you do, reach out to me personally and I will connect you with my contact there. Set up a time to speak here: *jonmac.co/apply*.

Always play the long game with your e-commerce store, because 6-12 months passes more quickly than you think. So get out there and scale up your ads and revenue each month. Investors prefer to see 20% average growth month after month. If you can show that and demonstrate stability, there's a good chance you could sell your store for a 7-figure payday.

Cash Flow Action Plan

1. How much do you want to sell your store for?

2. How much monthly profit will you need to reach that goal?

3. How many sales will you have to make to reach that goal?

4. How much ad spend will you need to reach that goal?

A Final Note

CASH FLOW FOR LIFE

Congrats, you made it! You've learned how to open, run, and sell your own online business! Thank you for sticking with me during this journey. I know there was a lot of information to take in, so I suggest you read the book several times and take notes. Feel free to review each chapter as you start your e-commerce business, step-by-step.

Now that you've finished the book, what will you do with all the knowledge, strategies, and techniques you've learned? What type of store are you going to launch? Which niches and products are you going to run campaigns for?

Are you ready to start (or continue, if you've been working along with each chapter) your journey to cash flow for life?

Before you put down this book and get to work, I highly recommend you continue reading, because I've put together some bonus reports for you that will serve as cheat sheets to help get you started. Read through all the supplementary tips and take action. Get out there and make it happen!

The fact is, you could read this book many times over, but unless you take immediate action, everything you just learned will go to waste. Also, it's important not to get "shiny object syndrome" and move on to the next trend. Focus is paramount, and you need to put in the time to make this business work.

Work hard, but work smart. Outsource whenever possible and you can manage the rest. No problem or barrier is too difficult to overcome. Simply search Google or YouTube to find answers and advice on nearly any topic.

So I'm challenging you right now to get your store up and running within the next 14 days.

Can you do it? I know you can! Imagine starting to make sales this month! How would that change your life?

You will finally be able to quit your job, spend more time with your family, and be your own boss.

You will be able to live your dreams right now instead of when you retire at 65 or later.

The time is now to make a massive change in your life. But it takes perseverance, focus, and determination to succeed. Never give up! Keep pushing through your obstacles. Celebrate your successes early on to keep you motivated.

Before you continue with the rest of the book, take some time to complete a business plan. Write down the top ten tasks you will accomplish within the next 14 days to create your e-commerce business.

Use your responses to the action plans at the end of each chapter. Your goals should include tasks such as launching your store, researching products and niches, creating your Facebook Ads campaigns, or finding a coach or mentor to help you with your business.

CASH FLOW FOR LIFE BUSINESS PLAN

Write 10 business goals you will achieve within the next 14 days.

1. _____

2. _____

3. _____

4. _____

5. _____

6. _____

7. _____

8. _____

9. _____

10. _____

Allow this book to be your cheat sheet to help you through every step of your e-commerce business and earn CASH FLOW FOR LIFE.

Now that you have a plan in place for your own business, consider how to pass on this knowledge to your friends and family, or perhaps find a partner to help you launch your business.

In this book, you have the exact blueprint we use in our

business to earn 7 figures every year. It's a strategy guide to help you earn revenue and profit quickly.

But you need to believe in yourself and have a vision for your business. Always know where you want to go and chart your course to that goal.

The best is about to come with my bonus reports. Like my "20 Hot Niche Products" list with several best-selling products you can sell on your store. These reports will shorten your learning curve and show you what's working well in the marketplace right now.

I can offer you a complimentary 30-minute strategy call with my best coach to help you get on track and make sure you're building out your new business properly from Day 1.

Apply here for a call with us: *jonmac.co/apply*. Include your name and time zone so we can coordinate your strategy call via phone or Skype.

I hope you learned a great deal and are motivated to take action to achieve your ultimate life goals, dreams, and aspirations! Again, don't forget to continue and check out the bonus reports at the end of this book. You will find the tips and suggestions powerful for your business growth.

I hope this is just the beginning of our journey together, and that I can personally help you in the future with training, coaching, and live events. I enjoy teaching, and I love changing people's lives. Maybe you will be next!

Finally, I hope you found what you were looking for in this book and I wish you all the luck, success, love, happiness, and prosperity that life has to offer. I truly believe you have the strength, focus, and perseverance to pursue your dreams and to never give up.

Now get out there and sell something!

Sellable. Sustainable. Scalable.

Sincerely,

SUCCESS STORIES

Todd Croly:

I started to try and make money online about 20 years ago. I tried just about every single program out there and failed, but I never gave up.

I spent thousands of dollars on so many programs that promised so much and never made a dime.

16 months ago I came across another course about selling physical products online. Again, I was very skeptical about it, but said to myself this is the LAST course I will ever buy.

It was one of Jon Mac's first courses on Ecommerce. I started his 8-week course and turned around and made 12 times my investment in 8 weeks, all while working a full time job.

I was so excited to say the least! Then later this year in 2016, Jon came out with the Millionaire Challenge course.

The MC course walks you through everything step by step. Jon's videos have a "looking over his shoulder" style. You also get weekly calls with Jon that are absolutely priceless.

The thing that I like the most about Jon's teaching is he is always straight to the point. Jon is the real deal.

There are so many courses out there today about selling online, but I wouldn't trust anyone but Jon.

I do what he says and make a lot of money doing it. It's the best feeling ever! The MC course takes everything to the next level and I couldn't be happier at where I am today.

Thanks to Jon I am getting closer every day to quitting my full time job!

Chase Bowers:

When it comes to business mentors, Jon Mac is at the top of my list. I've had the pleasure of attending his online trainings and live workshops and his knowledge and experience in online marketing is incredible.

Think of it like this... Imagine that you know of someone who is already successful with their own Ecommerce businesses, excels at setting up systems that are able to be duplicated, understands how to use paid ads to scale traffic, knows the value of leveraging time by creating a team, is doing this day to day in his own business and knows the pitfalls and mistakes to avoid.

Now imagine that this person is willing to share what he has learned to help you leverage this knowledge in your own business and speed up your path to success. That's the benefit of knowing and learning from Jon Mac!

In fact, he impressed me so much that I reached out to Jon to work with me in my own Ecommerce business on a weekly basis and I feel confident in recommending Jon to my closest friends.

Claus Lauter:

Let me start saying that I've been working in online marketing since 2001, but never did run my own online shop.

Before I moved over to Shopify in 2015 I was already using Facebook ads with Teespring for more than a year and had some good results.

I started with Jon's course Profit Store Pro back in June 2015 and later that year became a member of his Inner Circle group. When the Millionaire Challenge came up in 2016 I decided to continue with Jon's coaching and have not regretted it.

My Shopify store has since made about $700,000 in revenue and I have had about 25,000 orders so far. I am currently busy moving from Shopify to the Jon's CommerceHQ platform to increase the conversion rate and profit margin.

The Millionaire Challenge gives an A-Z jump start for everyone who seriously wants to start an Ecommerce business with drop shipping.

Jon's training videos are easy to follow and guide step-by-step through the process. Most importantly Jon updates them frequently and as a MC member you can approach Jon at any time with questions.

The biggest benefit of being a member of the MC group are the weekly 1 to 1 coaching calls with Jon. He gives you tips and best practices ideas to make your shop/business work.

Important to note is that you still have to work your ass off. The results do not come on their own. Ecommerce is a tough business and Facebook is changing the rules constantly.

So be prepared to work hard, learn every day, test every day and fail a lot, but success will come if you are persistent and follow Jon's advice.

I run a couple of other businesses and running an Ecommerce shop with Facebook ads is a roller-coaster experience like any other business venture. If you are prepared for it and willing to work hard, you will reach your goals with Jon's help.

BTW: My girlfriend and I will start 2017 traveling the world for 18 months and with the business setup provided by Jon's courses we will be able to be Digital Nomads, meaning traveling and running a business from anywhere in the world.

So it is up to you to set your goals. Jon will help you to reach them.

Jack Scanlan:

I've been working with Jon for almost a year now. He has helped my business tremendously and continues to help me innovate and grow.

The first milestone he helped me achieve was selling over half a million dollars last holiday season.

Next, I crossed 7 figures in my business less than a year after we started working together.

And now, Jon is helping me achieve the next level, multiple seven figures.

If you get a chance to work with Jon, do it!

He is a great teacher and mentor when it comes to all things Facebook. He knows how to innovate, and grow your business.

And he will tailor everything to help YOUR business grow. Thanks Jon, you rock!

William T. McWilliams:

I thought I knew what being an entrepreneur meant, then I met Jon Mac and realized that being an entrepreneur is more than just finding hot products, throwing them on a website and sending traffic to it, expecting that everything would just go well and steadily improve without much concern.

That mentality is what caused me to struggle through the last eleven years failed attempt after failed attempt at starting my own steady online business. The going got rough and seemed impossible, I would give up and follow someone else.

My life literally shifted dramatically for the better when he helped me shift my mindset from one of expecting certainty to allowing uncertainty to flow, not letting that fear of uncertainty paralyze me and stop me from continuing to take action.

That mindset shift also brought me clarity, making it easy to stop the constant searching and purchasing of those beautiful, shiny objects. I was suddenly able to focus on my goal and ignore all the chatter of a thousand voices in my inbox, calling out to me. I was finally able to recognize who could help me achieve the lifestyle I was yearning for all these years.

Being an entrepreneur is never a smooth journey that you can simply sit back and enjoy the ride and never expect setbacks. The ebb and flow of this lifestyle can drive you mad and having a mentor is that vital step for anyone wanting to achieve their goals. I saw that Jon Mac was doing what I wanted to be doing and it was an easy decision for me to follow his advice and reach bolder goals than I ever dreamed possible.

Edgar Veytia:

To those of us who have immersed ourselves in this world of ecommerce, it seems massive and ubiquitous. The charts we see show exponential growth and the numbers posted by those who arrived ahead of us seem staggering. But, in the context of the world at large, Ecommerce is barely out of the novelty phase. It's still in its infancy, which makes it the most exciting time and place to be right now.

The rules of the game change daily and we're far from anything that even remotely looks like a peak. As any industry matures, rules and regulations kick in favor of the established players and raise the barriers to entry. That is not the case at all in ecommerce as the barriers to entry are low, the path to success can be incredibly short, and the rewards disproportionately huge.

But, the conditions that foster these opportunities are also riddled with challenges. The rules are being made up as we go and contradictions are everywhere. Your greatest challenges are not your competitors, not me or Jon Mac, or anyone else in this field. It is the unknown. How do you stay on top of changes that can affect your business and kill your momentum? Where do you turn to get the best information available? What's working today and what stopped working yesterday?

Shiny objects are everywhere that promise success faster, better, cheaper. Gurus and self-styled experts are never far behind. And as we know, every gold rush has its miners where some mine for gold and some mine the miners.

If you're like me, it all sounds great and if you're really like me, you've spent a lot of money accumulating software and courses, OTO-1s, 2s and 3s, upsells, downsells and everything in between!

After you've burned through a lot of cash on dead-end products and re-hashed advice, you begin to cut through the noise and if you're lucky you find reliable sources that are out in front that consistently produce results. They are few and far between and tend not to be the storefront variety that hocks the latest and greatest flavor of the week.

After a long, circuitous (read expensive) route, I came across Jon Mac. Jon's reputation preceded him so I was excited to hear what he had to say. And, learning from Jon, I'll get right to the point.

It was through Jon that I turned my first real dollar. Yes, I had made some money before. But, my criteria is that of a business person. A windfall, a transaction, even a series of transactions, regardless of how much money falls into your lap, doesn't mean it's a business. I set out to start a business and Jon set me on that course - a business that consistently produces results based on a system, the right tools and the right intel.

Jon provided me with all three.

Jon has a system. No nonsense. No fluff. Follow the logic, follow the plan and barring the usual caveats, you'll make money. More importantly, you'll have a business. And, more important than that - you'll have a business that makes money!

Jon has great tools. He has been at this long enough and at a large enough scale that he can test to levels the rest of us cannot even approximate. Part of Jon's success is his methodical approach, continually A/B testing and sniffing out best practices and incorporating them into his approach.

Jon has cutting edge intel. In this continually changing world where Facebook, our main advertising platform, is constantly tweaking their algorithms, the difference between success and failure, profit or loss, often hinges on knowing what you don't know. By the time word gets around and circulates like a game of "telephone" through all the groups, what we hear too often is a lot of rehash, spin and contradiction. Jon finds what's working, tests it, repeats and tests some more, and then you're the first to know. You hear it directly from Jon.

There are many successful ecommerce entrepreneurs. Most go along quietly minding their own business which is fine, but a few make the decision to turn around and give back to others, the way they were mentored by the best before them. Jon is one of those who decided to give back and as long as he's willing to let others in on his system, the winning move is to seize the opportunity. A good mentor is a life changer. Jon is the real deal.

Zach Winsett:

Prior to joining Jon Mac's Millionaire Challenge I was only doing online marketing for local businesses. I had heard of Shopify and E-commerce through Website Magazine and how the Ecommerce industry was skyrocketing. I decided to join the Millionaire Challenge because of Jon Mac's experience and how he could put me on the fast track to success. This fast track could not have happened at a better time for me as I was laid off from work just weeks earlier. I quickly absorbed his training and put it into action.

Just three days after joining his program I launched my first Shopify store. I struggled in the beginning finding the best products to add to my store and Jon assisted me with finding proven products to place into my store. I quickly learned that the struggle with finding products was just beginning and I needed to learn Facebook ads. Jon could tell me exactly what was working at that moment with Facebook ads and how I could tweak my ads to squeeze out more return. Still I struggled and that is where the coaching calls with Jon helped the most. He assisted me with setting up my Facebook ad manager dashboard so that I only focused on the data that mattered.

It took me awhile to get a firm grasp on all of the systems and techniques but just a few short months later I celebrated my first 100k in sales from a single Shopify store. I then celebrated my next 75k within a two-month span.

If you are looking for ways to generate cash online, you certainly need to look at Jon Mac's training programs and dive straight in. Besides training you also must have the desire to take action. I recommend that you implement the steps within the videos as you watch them. Also watch the videos a second time to make sure you have everything completed. Take each step as a task and before you know it you will have your store online.

Always keep an open mind with Facebook ads, you must develop the mindset of testing various ads even when your budget gets tight. I did not have a lot of money for Facebook ads when I first started. Remember, I had been laid off and my main income stream was severed. Start small and then reinvest the first profits back into creating more Facebook ads.

Above all, do not get discouraged or give-up. This is a real business and it should be treated as one. If you treat it as a hobby, you will get paid like a hobby.

Good luck to your E-commerce business and I look forward to hearing about your success.

20 GREATEST ENTREPRENEUR SECRETS

1. **Invest in a coach or mentor.**

   This strategy alone will save you thousands of dollars and years of time. Learn from mentors' successes and avoid their mistakes.

2. **Join a mastermind group.**

   Networking with other like-minded entrepreneurs is essential for growing your business and finding out what's currently working in the marketplace.

3. **Include your family.**

   Can you find a way for your partner to help you with your business? Do they complement one of your strengths or weaknesses? It's important to include them and get their support.

4. **Take calculated risks.**

   All true success comes with some amount of risk, so take care in calculating your risks wisely to improve your chance of winning.

5. **Stay healthy throughout your journey.**

   Could you stand to lose a few pounds? Do you exercise at least 30 minutes per day? The more active you are, the less stressed you will be. Your health can have a huge effect on your business.

6. **Surround yourself with successful people.**

   They say your income will equal the average income of your 5 closest friends. So choose your friends wisely. Make friends with other entrepreneurs who share your dreams, goals, and vision.

7. **Invest in yourself with online courses.**

   You should continue learning throughout your life. Stay ahead of the curve with your marketing and business strategies by learning from others who have "cracked the code".

8. **Eliminate failure from your vocabulary.**

You never fail in life; you only learn. Gather valuable data each time you test out a new campaign and learn something new about what did or didn't work.

9. **Outsource wherever possible.**

   If you can't perform a certain task or don't have enough time, hire a sub-contractor to handle the day-to-day operations of your business.

10. **Find joint venture partners.**

    They say two heads are better than one, and it's always helpful to have someone to bounce ideas off of. Partner with another entrepreneur who complements your talents.

11. **Pay your team ASAP.**

    Keep your team happy by paying them on time so they don't have to worry about getting a paycheck. This will help optimize their performance.

12. **Leverage weekends.**

    As an entrepreneur, you will not have a normal work schedule at the start, so take advantage of this and work on weekend mornings before everyone else in your household wakes up.

13. **Eliminate time-wasting activities.**
    Instead of watching Netflix or television, use this
    extra time to focus on the growth of your business.
    Remember, it's all about the long game and building
    yourself a real asset.

14. **Study other successful entrepreneurs.**
    Read biographies of famous people such as Sir
    Richard Branson, Elon Musk, and Steve Jobs. Get
    inspired to take action!

15. **Focus on branding your company.**
    Branding will become significantly more important
    within the next 5 years. Be sure to stay in the
    forefront of your customers' minds and maintain
    a good reputation with your business so they keep
    coming back for more.

16. **Apply the 3xT+3xM=30xROI rule.**
    This equation represents the fact that success in
    business takes 3 times longer than you think it will
    and costs 3 times more than budgeted, but will net

30 times the return on your investment.

17. **Use the sales success formula.**

   People buy from referrals most often, and will only buy from people they know, like, and trust. So develop this relationship early on with your customers.

18. **Apply the Rule of 7.**

   Napoleon Hill says, "It takes seven bits of communication between buyer and seller in order for a sale to close." This is where retargeting comes into play.

19. **Remember that the fortune is made in the follow-up.**

   Keep in constant contact with your customers by emailing them weekly with fresh promotions to increase your LTV and AOV.

20. **Never give up…ever!**

   It's harder to quit and start again than to endure the journey. Believe in yourself, your vision, and your passion, and you will succeed!

10 NEW BUSINESS MUST-DOs

1. Be so passionate and obsessed with this business that you have sleepless nights thinking about your store and campaigns.

2. Be willing to sacrifice your free time—hanging out with friends, watching TV, playing sports, or other leisurely activities—to focus on your business entirely, day in and day out.

3. Secure an experienced accountant and bookkeeper early on for your business so you are organized and understand where you're headed.

4. Keep your day job as long as possible while running your business on the side, using your income as seed money until you have enough saved up to take the full-time entrepreneur plunge.

5. Rely on emotional support from your partner or spouse to prepare for the long hours that come with

being an entrepreneur.

6. Know your target niche market intimately. Read their conversations on social media, visit websites they browse, and understand their buying behaviors.

7. Align yourself with those who are smarter, and who have more experience and a bigger network.

8. Retain 51% or more ownership of your business so you will never lose control to angel investors down the road if you choose that path.

9. Work from home as long as possible without paying for office space to save thousands per month on overhead and expenses.

10. Make your store unique as compared to your competition so people remember you when they visit your website.

25 HOT NICHE PRODUCTS

You can find all these items on AliExpress.com.

BRACELETS

Bohemian Style Silver Cuff
  Bangle
Grandma Love Leather Bracelet
Native Dream Catcher Bracelet
Unconditional Love Autism
  Bracelet

NECKLACES

Buck and Doe Necklace
Daddy's Girl Dog Tag Necklace
Glow In The Dark Necklace
Heart Choker Necklace
I Love You I Know Necklace
Lil Sis Mom Big Sis Necklace
Mother Daughter Necklaces
Owl Tree Necklace
T-Rex Skeleton Necklace
Zodiac Moon Necklace

EARRINGS

Crystal Skull Earrings
Guardian Angel Earrings
Wine Opener Earrings

RINGS

Gold Jesus Ring
Ohm Symbol Yoga Ring

OTHER

3D Wine iPhone Cover
Biker Skull Mask
Dog Collar Night Safety Light
Firefights Vinyl Sticker Car
  Decal
Mini Tactical Flashlight
Survival Whistle

15 STORE OPTIMIZATION TIPS

1. **Use a promotional black bar on the top of your store's home page.**

    This promo bar will inform your customers about your current offers such as Free Shipping, 50% OFF, and Buy 2, Get 1 Free.

2. **Display photos of real people wearing your products.**

    Invest in a photoshoot with models and a professional photographer to add class to your store.

3. **Confirm regularly that your store is 100% mobile-optimized.**

    Test your store weekly on iPhone and Android phones to ensure all the elements are loading properly and page load speed is fast.

4. **Include a bulk order page.**

   You might be surprised how many people want to order in bulk. Create a simple page with a contact form that sends their message to bulk@yourdomain. com so you can offer them a special deal.

5. **Do not neglect your About Us page.**

   New customers might not know your brand or company, so make sure you have a detailed About Us page describing your products and showcasing how amazing they are.

6. **Build intuitive navigation.**

   People shouldn't have a hard time finding the search box or your catalog page and should be able to check out within just a few clicks.

7. **Display regular price on your product page.**

   With sales such as 50% OFF, show regular prices and cross them out so people know the value they're getting.

8. **Format your Buy button big and bold.**

   Divert your customers' attention to the Buy button

with catchy formatting. Split test different colors, but make sure it's large enough so it really stands out.

9. **Photograph product images so they appear clean and bright.**
    Take professional detailed images of your products so people can clearly see what they are buying. Multiple angle shots highlighting different features will help to increase conversion.

10. **Use color swatches where possible.**
    Round, color icon buttons on mobile apps will provide a more seamless checkout and shopping experience. Avoid drop-down menus, which are more cumbersome.

11. **Incorporate credit card and security logos.**
    Establish rapport and trust with your customers by displaying familiar logos such as Visa, MasterCard, Norton, and McAfee.

12. **Display your store phone number prominently.**
    Having a phone number people can call and leave a message for you is helpful for establishing trust.

13. **Display customer reviews on your product pages and cart page.**

    People will feel more comfortable buying when they see that others have had good experiences with your products.

14. **Post on social media channels daily.**

    Social media sites include Instagram, Facebook, Twitter, Snapchat. The more you post, the more you'll reach customers and prospects. Hold contests and giveaways for greater engagement.

15. **Design a checkout process that is quick and easy.**

    Split the checkout process into 2 or 3 pages or sections so it looks less intimidating to customers. This also allows you to capture their email addresses for abandon cart recovery later, if they decide not to buy and for direct mail marketing.

15 WAYS TO OPTIMIZE YOUR ADS

1. **Separate mobile and desktop ads.**

   It's best practice to separate mobile and desktop ads, so you can optimize your budgets and conversions based on specific devices.

2. **Separate desktop newsfeed and right-side ads.**

   Similarly, it's important to separate out placements to clearly see where you are making sales and then scale your budgets accordingly.

3. **Split test product images.**

   You never know what is going to trigger a sale with your customers. Images are the most powerful way to split test and obtain higher click-through rates and lower costs per sale.

4. **Split test calls to action.**

   Find out which calls to action work best with your

particular niche and customers. Try different offers such as LAST CHANCE! or FREE SHIPPING NEXT 24 HOURS!

5. **Segment out your interests.**
The best way to accomplish this is to test different interest groups with your ads. For example, magazine interests could go in one ad set, associations in another, and website interests in a third.

6. **Use website conversion campaigns.**
The most profitable way to run Facebook Ads is with the purchase pixel and website conversion optimization campaigns.

7. **Track your profits and losses daily.**
Create and update a spreadsheet with your sales, ad spend, revenue, profit, and ROI daily so you know exactly how your business is performing.

8. **Target lookalike audiences.**
Lookalike audiences can be highly profitable when used with your ads. Create them from the custom audience of a specific product page, after at least

1,000 people have visited the page.

9. **Retarget your past buyers.**

   Many store owners don't retarget, yet it's one of the most profitable ad types out there. Show your current customers additional products they might be interested in and watch how high your ROI rises.

10. **Identify profitable age groups.**

   You might find that one age group (EX: 25-34) is much more profitable than the others. Consider breaking out this ad by itself if it does much better.

11. **Identify profitable mobile devices.**

   Compare iPhone vs Android phones in your Facebook Reporting details to determine which type is more profitable for you. Break the winner out into its own ad.

12. **Apply flex targeting.**

   Layer different combinations of interests together to test whether you are reaching the most passionate fans in your niche. Target people who Like "X" and "Y" and "Z".

13. **Duplicate to win.**

    Duplicate your most profitable ads 3 times per day at different budgets to see whether you can get more reach out of a campaign.

14. **Scale your budgets on winning ads.**

    Slowly adjust the budgets by 25% for your most profitable ads, once per day in the morning.

15. **Aim for double return on ad spend.**

    You should at least be doubling your ad spend with revenue daily. If not, pause any low-performing ads after 24 hours.

FANTASTIC AD EXAMPLE

Look at the amazing Facebook Ad below. It received more than 500,000 Likes, 177,000 Shares, and 59,000 Comments, going viral. These store owners likely made seven figures on this one product.

Their use of a 50% OFF promotion and scarcity (Mother's Day Cutoff: April 24) helped boost this post tremendously. Notice that the owner replied to all comments one by one with a link to buy, driving even more traffic to their store.

7 STEPS TO LEAVING YOUR JOB

1. **Eliminate your worst fear.**

   Most entrepreneurs were initially terrified to leave their comfortable 9-5, salaried jobs in pursuit of freedom. But what's your worst fear? That you might not succeed? One solution is to build your business on the side for 3-6 months to prove that it's sustainable before quitting your day job.

2. **Get your finances in order.**

   You need to be in a good financial position before quitting your job. I recommend at least 3-6 months of savings before you quit.

3. **Kick self-doubt to the curb.**

   You might not think you are smart enough, experienced enough, or prepared enough to quit your job, but there will never be a perfect time to do it. You just have to believe in yourself and your abilities, and you will find a way to become successful on your own.

4.   **Look through a different lens.**
If you tell people about your plans to quit and start your own business, you will probably get a lot of blank stares and weird looks. From a young age, we are programmed to attend school, find a decent job, and climb the corporate ladder, then retire at 65 with a government pension.

Do you really want to work your entire life just to curl up and die afterwards? Your fear of quitting comes from this societal norm. People think that having a 9-5 job means job security. But the truth is, being employed by someone else is just as risky as running a business because you could be let go at any time.

5.   **Imagine the worst that could happen.**
They say something ventured and lost is better than nothing ventured at all. This is so true when it comes to taking the risk to become your own boss.

If you don't make it work, what's the worst that could happen? You could return to a 9-5 job, no big deal. But don't you owe it to yourself to at least try? You only have one life to live. Don't waste it!

6. **Set a deadline.**

   Studies show that when you set and write down deadlines, you are much more likely to reach your goals. We are creatures of habit and some of us tend to do things last-minute. But before quitting your job, you should set a hard date. Know how much money you need to save before you quit.

7. **Break out of your comfort zone.**

   You'd like to quit your job, but it seems as if you have to climb Mount Everest first to get there. It's so much easier to sit on your couch watching TV night after night, or party and spend all the money you earned from the prior week. Make the decision to change your life for the better. Push yourself out of your comfort zone!

ABOUT THE AUTHOR

JON MAC is an international entrepreneur, author, speaker and coach for eCommerce and Facebook Ads™. He first discovered his entrepreneur DNA at the age of 15, when he hosted dance parties for 250 to 500 people, DJing live on stage, and (surprisingly) earning a decent income from it.

Jon has taught thousands of entrepreneurs how to build, operate, scale, and sell their e-commerce stores using Shopify and Facebook Ads.

As an e-commerce coach, Jon has mentored and been mentored by several 7-figure earners during the past 5 years. The systems and strategies he learned and used are outlined in this book.

Originally from Vancouver, BC, Canada, Jon studied business and marketing at the University of British Columbia until 2006. He lived in the Toronto area for more than 6 years, where he met his fiancée, Jacqueline. They currently live in Kelowna, BC.

THE MILLIONAIRE CHALLENGE

Feeling overwhelmed by all the information in this book? Gain clarity and begin your journey with step-by-step video training in Jon's new program, The Millionaire Challenge.

Jon has taken several people from zero to 7 figures within months, and you could be his next success story! Get unlimited access to Jon via email and Skype for a full 12 months and watch your business grow to 7 figures.

Jon will simplify the process for you, help you optimize your business, and guide you to choose winning, profitable products right from Day One. This will potentially save you tens of thousands of dollars wasted on testing. Let Jon show you the way and give you all his best strategies that are proven to work in the current marketplace!

If you want personalized, one-on-one help and coaching from Jon Mac, contact him directly at *jonmac.co/apply*. However, Jon's time is extremely limited, so he can only take on a certain number of students each year.

So, if you want to skyrocket your success by running your own e-commerce store and have Jon support you the entire way, book a call with him now!

For more information, visit ***jonmac.co/apply***.

Now that you've finished this book, we would love to hear from you! What did you like? What didn't you like? What can we improve for the next edition? But most importantly, tell us where you are in your e-commerce journey. Let us know if you hit any snags and need any help. We love working one-on-one with people like you!

COMMERCE HQ

Get ready for the most groundbreaking e-commerce software platform to ever hit the market. COMMERCE HQ will soon take the industry by storm, offering unlimited stores, one-click upsells, and an incredible drag-and-drop, visual store builder.

This is going to be a game changer that will allow you to scale out multiple niche stores with the click of a button. Increase your store revenues by 300% using one-click upsells to funnel your visitors into buying more products.

If you want the most powerful platform out there for the highest converting store themes, get your copy of COMMERCE HQ now. You will not find an easier e-commerce platform to help you get started on your journey. We provide numerous step-by-step videos and checklists to ensure you're squeezing every dollar of profit from your product campaigns.

COMMERCE HQ was built for marketers, by marketers, who know what does and doesn't work when it comes to conversion optimization. You will never have to worry about low ROI or conversion rates again. Get on this professional marketing platform today!

For more information, visit CommerceHQ.com.

GLOSSARY

Add to Cart	Button a customer selects to add an item to the shopping cart of an online store
ads	In Facebook, they contain ad image and ad copy
ad sets	In Facebook, they contain demographics, device placement, and bidding options for targeting
ad spend	Amount a company spends on advertisements
autoresponder	Email software that automatically sends messages to a list of customers
average order value (AOV)	Average amount people pay per order
brand	A company's overall look and feel, including logo, website design, and ads
broad ads	Ads targeted to broad categories of customers; audience size typically larger than for precise ads

buyers list	List of email addresses for a company's customers
Campaigns	In Facebook, these contain optimization objectives (EX: clicks to website, website conversion, page post engagement)
checkout	Page on a site where customers purchase products; also, the process of checking out items
click-through rate (CTR)	Percentage of people who clicked on an ad
conversion rate (CR)	Percentage of people who buy compared to people who simply visit a store
cost per action (CPA)	Amount it costs to make a sale with an ad
cost per click (CPC)	Amount it costs per click on an ad
coupon code	A discount off original product price
CPM (cost per mille)	Cost per thousand impressions; how much it costs for 1,000 people to view an ad
cross-sell	Offer different products to customers via emails and retargeting ads

custom audience	Group created from people who visit a particular product page
demographics	Details such as age, gender, or location for a target audience
drop ship	Process of ordering a product from China that ships directly to customers in the US
ePacket	Preferred (faster) shipping option in AliExpress; averages 2 weeks for delivery in US
Facebook page	Location where a company posts store ads
Free Plus Shipping	Offer where a product itself is free, but a customer pays shipping charges (EX: $9.95)
fulfilment	Process of ordering products from vendors (EX: AliExpress) to be sent to customers who order from a store
funnel	Series of product offers presented to leads, prospects, or current customers

giveaway	Free product to entice people into a sales funnel
intersect	Layer two or more levels of interests; for example, people who like "hunting" AND "fishing"
lead	Person who has visited a store but did not make a purchase
lead magnet	Free product to entice people into a sales funnel
lifetime value (LTV)	Average amount a typical customer pays over 12 months
lookalike	Audience similar to people who previously visited a particular store; Facebook automatically generates this data using special algorithms
loss leader	Free product to entice people into a sales funnel
margin	Amount of net profit made from a sale after ad spend and fulfillment cost are subtracted
multi-variate test	Split test multiple design elements on a store to see which combination converts into higher sales

niche	Small, specific segment of the market (EX: hunters or avid readers)
optimize	Marketing tactics to ensure the best sales, such as pausing unprofitable ads or increasing budgets on profitable ads
outsource	Hire virtual assistant(s) to perform daily operations for a business
page post engagement (PPE)	Campaign where Facebook shows ads to people most likely to Like, Comment, or Share an ad
precise ads	Ads targeted to people with specific interests; audience typically smaller (< 500k) than for broad ads
Project Manager	Virtual assistant hired to manage a team who reports directly to the owner
promotional calendar	Organizing ad campaigns based on holidays and events throughout the year
purchase pixel	Facebook image used to track ad sales
reach	Number of people exposed to a particular ad

reengage	Process of replying to comments on ad posts with a link to buy a product
Reports	Feature within Facebook Ads Manager that details ad statistics
retarget	Process of showing ads to people who visited a store in the past
return on ad spend (ROAS)	Amount of revenue made from a Facebook ad spend
return on investment (ROI)	Amount calculated by dividing profit by ad spend (after fulfillment costs)
revenue	Amount made from ad sales
reverse engineer	Technique of viewing other companies' ad campaigns and products to leverage for another store
right-hand side (RHS)	Ad placement on right side of Facebook Newsfeed
scale	Increase ad budget or create additional ads to increase overall ad spend on an account
split test	Compare two or more similar ads to determine which one is more profitable

traffic	Visitors to a website
trip wire	Free product to entice people into a sales funnel
upsell	Offer customers products similar to items already purchased, via emails and retargeting ads
vendor	Company who provides and sells products for customer fulfillment
virtual assistant (VA)	Worker hired to assist with daily tasks; often from other countries for cost-efficiency
website conversion	Campaign where Facebook displays ads to people who are most likely to buy

ONLINE RESOURCES

Active Campaign	www.activecampaign.com
AliExpress	www.aliexpress.com
Arqspin	www.arqspin.com
AWeber	www.aweber.com
ClickFunnels	www.clickfunnels.com
Commerce HQ	www.commercehq.com
Empire Flippers	www.empireflippers.com
Fiverr	www.fiverr.com
Hotjar	www.hotjar.com
Instagram	www.instagram.com
MailChimp	www.mailchimp.com
Pinterest	www.pinterest.com
Qwaya	www.qwaya.com
Shopify	www.shopify.com
Skype	www.skype.com
Snapchat	www.snapchat.com
Stripe	www.stripe.com
Trello	www.trello.com
Twitter	www.twitter.com
Upwork	www.upwork.com
VWO	www.vwo.com